JOURNEY TO THE GREEN AND GOLDEN LANDS

There were no corner drug stores on the Oregon and California Trails!

The great westward trek of those hardy pioneers of the 1840s is a saga of courage and fortitude. The daily struggles to survive against even the minor (by modern standards) ailments as toothaches, broken limbs, diarrhea, assumed major proportions to those hardy but ill-equipped pioneers.

How they coped with these and other medical and physical problems is a chronicle of stamina. Even so the plains were dotted with thousands of graves.

Dr. Doetsch, a microbiologist by profession, and a student of American history by avocation, regales the reader with accurate and vivid descriptions of the myriad hazards faced by these brave people. More than two years of research into the diaries kept by some of the more literate souls (and some not so literate but mindful of their place in history) produces an engrossing story of their everyday existence— what they ate, how they dressed, what they did for amusement . . . and how they survived during the long march westward.

JOURNEY TO THE GREEN AND GOLDEN LANDS

All the past we leave behind,
We debouch upon a newer mightier world, varied world,
Fresh and strong the world we seize, world of labor and the march,
Pioneers! O pioneers!

Walt Whitman

Raymond N. Doetsch

JOURNEY TO THE GREEN AND GOLDEN LANDS

THE EPIC OF SURVIVAL ON THE WAGON TRAIL

National University Publications
KENNIKAT PRESS   //   1976
Port Washington, N. Y.   //   London

Manufactured in the United States of America

Published by
Kennikat Press Corp.
Port Washington, N.Y./London

Library of Congress Cataloging in Publication Data

Doetsch, Raymond Nicholas, 1920–
    Journey to the green and golden lands.

    Bibliography: p.
    Includes index.
    1. Overland journeys to the Pacific. 2. Medicine–The West–History. 3. The West–History–1848–1950. I. Title.
F593.D62   917.8'04'2   76-8433
ISBN 0-8046-9142-8

CONTENTS

ACKNOWLEDGMENTS

Sincere appreciation is expressed to the following publishers for extending their permission to quote excerpts from copyright materials: Bobbs-Merrill for Douglas T. Miller's *The Birth of Modern America;* California Historical Society for I. D. Paden's (editor) *The Journal of Madison Berryman Mooreman;* Columbia University Press for G. W. Read and R. Gaines's (editors) *Gold Rush: The Journals, Drawings, and other papers of J[oseph] Goldsborough Bruff;* Doubleday for R. Dunlop's *Doctors of the American Frontier;* Harper & Row for R. A. Billington's *The Far Western Frontier;* University of Kentucky Press for E. D. Perkins's *Gold Rush Diary;* Alfred A. Knopf for Nancy Wilson Ross's *Westward the Women;* Macmillan for I. D. Paden's *In the Wake of the Prairie Schooner;* University Microfilms for A. J. Delano's *Life on the Plains and among the Diggings;* W. W. Norton for H. E. Sigerist's *American Medicine;* Old West Publishing Company for D. L. Morgan's (editor) *The Overland Diary of James A. Pritchard;* Oregon Historical Society for J. Ball's *Across the Continent Seventy Years Ago,* J. Minto's *Reminiscences of Honorable John Minto, Pioneer of 1844,* and *Letters of Peter H. Burnett;* Prentice-Hall for E. Dick's *The Sod House Frontier, 1854–1890;* and G. P. Putnam for H. R. Driggs's *Westward America.*

JOURNEY TO THE GREEN AND GOLDEN LANDS

INTRODUCTION

In contrast to numerous excellent accounts of political, social, and economic features of great migrations, the medical and physical problems of pioneers traveling the Oregon and Overland trails in the 1840s have been given but scant attention by historians. Americans may be reminded today, as we note the two hundredth anniversary of our country's founding, that they come from sterner stuff than they realize by recalling the fortitude of ordinary people confronted with survival problems that make modern ones look simple.

Rarely, if ever, did a man in the watered and forested East need to worry about thirst and dehydration, heat stroke and prostration, alkali poisoning, enervation and extreme fatigue, over-exposure to wet and cold, and recurring threats of gunshot wounds, drowning, severe sprains, and broken bones. Nor was he exposed to little nagging problems and ailments, never before thought about very much, which became ever more insistent and loomed ever larger during the five months (or more) trek: continually sunburned and cracked skin, especially of the fingers, lips, and nose; blistered, bruised, and sore feet; strained backs and torn ligaments; open and festering wounds that refused to heal; dust inhalation; sore and sun-blinded eyes; snake bites; insects, vermin, and lice; ordinary laundry, toilet, and simple hygienic routines like hair and teeth care; washing and bathing; the preparation and preservation of food; childbirth; burial; treatment and care of the seriously ill in a constantly jostling prairie schooner; and the ever-mounting psychological pressures and mental abrasions—a pathology of events induced by exposure to trials and encounters never before met with or imagined.

When to be a good Samaritan, when a Levite? When to abandon a wagon with its occupants dying from some mysterious and awesome disease? When to assume the additional, and perhaps fatal, burden of a mother and her children when she had lost all else? When to share the last bit of food and drop of water, and when to hoard it? Inextricably linked to the need for making soul-rending decisions was the ever-present fact of the trail. Physical details of climate, topography, waters, vegetation, and animal life, not only served as the stage and backdrop on which daily dramas unfolded but were their key features, and the emigrants responded to them consciously or unconsciously, day by day, hour by hour. For some emigrant trains the journey overland was long and hard but not extraordinary, whereas for others it became a tragic last venture.

It is the main purpose of this account to describe how early trans-Mississippi travelers to Oregon and California prepared for their journey, carried out their daily tasks, and responded to the various physical stresses and challenges that confronted them in the context of the wagon train setting. It is a tale of good luck and bad, coincidence, excitement, and boredom, tragic and happy endings. But intimate personal items and specifics of treatments for various accidents and ailments are rarely given in accounts of life on the trail, and our image of the sequence of events must be speculative to some degree. Only a relatively few medically trained persons wrote about their trail experiences; the bulk of available material was written by laymen of various degrees of literacy and education.

The story told here is related in the light of medical practice, in both its "professional" and folk forms, as it existed in the 1840s. The influence of American popular culture in the age of Jackson and the prevailing morality of the times also are recognized. It is an interesting and complex story involving the challenge of the land, nineteenth-century culture, and American medicine, during a transitional stage in our history. There was an interaction among all these elements that made the events considered here fascinating.

Let us begin by meeting the participants.

1

THE EMIGRANTS

The trans-Mississippi pioneers of the 1840s went west for reasons as varied as themselves. There were farmers and their families, trappers, vagabonds, adventurers, political crusaders, fugitives from justice, failures, sick people seeking health, and missionaries—among others. Hulbert's imagined summary of the "Golden Army" of 1849 wealth seekers included:[1]

... rich men, poor men, beggar men, thieves, farmers, lawyers, doctors, merchants, preachers, workmen, Republicans, Whigs, Federalists, Abolitionists, Baptists, Methodists, Transcendentalists, Campbellites, Millerites, Presbyterians, Mormons, white men, black men, yellow men, Germans, Russians, Poles, Chileans, Swiss, Spaniards, sailors, steamboat men, lumbermen, gamblers, the loose, squint-eyed, pockmarked, one-armed, the bearded, the beardless, the mustachioed, side-whiskered, and goateed, singing, cursing, weeping, and laughing in their sleep.

There were more emigrants from the farm than from the city, not only because factory workers and shopkeepers probably could not readily imagine themselves as frontier farmers, but in 1840 approximately ninety persons out of every hundred among 17 million citizens of the United States lived on farms or in a rural setting. While some emigrants hoped to establish themselves in business, a trade, or politics, the country was mainly a nation of small farmers of mostly English, Scotch, and Welsh ancestry and temperament. Farming did not lend itself to the accumulation of great fortunes, but many a man followed doggedly in the footsteps of his forefathers in clinging to the land.

---

[1]   A. B. Hulbert, *The Forty-Niners: The Chronicle of the California Trail*, p. 6.

Fig. 1   A highly romanticized version of trans-Mississippi
          pioneers by Emanuel Leutze titled *Westward the
          Course of Empire Takes Its Way.* Courtesy of
          National Collection of Fine Arts, Smithsonian
          Institution.

The financial panic of 1837 had more severe and long-lasting effects on the Middle West than on the East, mainly because the former had launched numerous and ill-conceived schemes of town building, land speculation, railroad construction, and banking ventures, in the confident expectation that boom times were certain to arrive soon. The depression brought, among other things, a severe drop in the price of farm products, and undoubtedly many a farmer and his family, discouraged and puzzled by economic developments beyond their understanding, looked westward for a fresh start. Economic considerations alone would probably not have induced the great migrations of the 1840s; there were political, religious, and social reasons, too. Economics was important, especially when wheat sold for ten cents a bushel and bacon was so cheap that steamboats used it for fuel.

After the decision to go west was finally made, after all the preparations were completed, and just on the eve of starting off on the plains, gnawing doubts about the undertaking assailed many an emigrant's mind. Some were worried sick, some were frightened, and most were probably anxious and nervous about what the future held. A lot of them had a funny feeling in their stomachs, whether or not they admitted it.

There were stories about Indians, stampedes, the terrific heat and lack of water, bad accidents, mysterious sicknesses, and a hundred other vague and worrisome things. A man might question his judgment as to whether he really was doing right. Perhaps it would be better to wait a year and see how others made out. Of course, all or many of the choice spots might be taken by then, but this could not really happen, could it?

They had bad dreams sometimes. How would a wife and children, especially the babies, stand up to a five months trip in the open country? What if the food ran out? Should one of the new cut-offs be tried? What if something went wrong with the wagon, or the oxen, or someone in the family—would anyone help? No. One had to depend on oneself; everyone would be too busy and probably have troubles and problems of his own—maybe even worse than imagined. Still, it was wise to try to join up with a good bunch if you could, preferably people you knew.

Some wondered whether they should have tried a little harder before they gave up on their farms. Many, though, had worked themselves ragged and bone-tired, and still ended up with nothing to show

for their efforts but large debts, calloused hands, and prematurely aged
bodies. You worked like a dog, and ended up living like a dog—even
worse. Then leave it all behind—no turning back; one couldn't turn
back, there wasn't any place to go back to now!

Some wondered whether the stakes weren't too high for gambling.
All life's savings tied up in a wagon and a few critters pulling it. All
life's personal possessions (and not many of them either!) in one or a
few square boxes on wheels—if they go, there goes the whole shebang!
Was it worth the risk?

There was no doubt about it, one just *had* to make it to Oregon
or California . . . to those green and golden lands where life was supposed to be kinder and easier, and where the children would be a lot better
off, too—or so it was dreamed. There were a lot of other fellows in the
same boat, and there was no use being too gloomy right at the start—at
least it was best not to let it show.

The virgin soil, the towering snow-topped mountains, the buffalo
and antelope, the awesome scenery, and the vast, silent, primordial
open country beckoned. Freedom, real or imagined, from the conven-
tions and fetters of the old society, and maybe a chance to make a fortune, lured emigrants toward the Pacific shore. In the West one might
readily believe that all men were created equal, and that the fertile land
and its treasures were practically free for the taking since there were no
proprietors or landlords. Some probably remembered that even so, the
land would still have to be cultivated, crops planted, business established, Indians fought, and much hard work be done before the profits
rolled in.

The notion developed that America, its democratic system, its
Protestant Christianity, and its way of life, were the hope of the world.
It seemed only natural that the destiny of America should be to expand
to the Pacific Ocean, and although philosophical notions such as that of
freedom might have motivated some people, the West mainly represent-
ed fertile, new, free land, and with it the hope of prosperity. In general, however, it was not the completely destitute man that went west,
because some money was needed for travel, for investing in equipment
and supplies, and for setting up in the new land. It has been estimated
that in 1843, for example, an outlay of between seven hundred and
fifteen hundred dollars was required to purchase the oxen, wagons, and
supplies needed to go from the Missouri River to the coast.

The emigrants brought their culture with them—tools, techniques, medicines, as well as their laws, politics, prejudices, and superstitions. Important things in the American scheme, such as practicality, egalitarianism, invincibility, individualism, and bigness also were brought west, together with personalities and temperaments, foibles, and bodily infirmities.

That coarseness and strength combined with acuteness and inquisitiveness, that practical, inventive turn of mind, quick to find expedients, that masterful grip of material things, lacking in artistic but powerful to effect great ends, that restless, nervous energy, that dominant individualism, working for good and for evil, and withal that buoyancy and exuberance which comes with freedom, these are the traits of the frontier . . . [2]

The fat and thin, clever and stupid, sanguine and choleric, overnourished and underfed, dyspeptic and tubercular, nearsighted and far, all journeyed west, carrying with them that which was inseparable from them.

The emigrants of the 1840s launched themselves from the banks of the Missouri River into a region as unknown and dangerous to them as that the first astronauts met with upon landing on the moon. These early pioneers would be beaten and pounded and molded into new shapes and attitudes by the ordeal of the trail, as if on a giant anvil. With the myriad pressures and hazards of their new environment, their bodies and minds, and all else, would have to adapt, or shatter into bits and pieces along the way—to be quickly covered over and forgotten.

Yet, for all the apparent external adaptations, there was a consistency, too, and after the trail experiences American culture in the West more often than not reflected older eastern patterns. It has been suggested that Americans might have considered themselves immune to, or absolved from, the influences of historical time by being expansionists, embodying thereby the idea of a continued renewal going back to Jefferson's time. But if historical tensions were alleviated, others were created, and some believed that the rapid settlement of the West during the first half of the nineteenth century weakened earlier institutions of

---

[2]   F.J. Turner, "The Significance of the Frontier in American History," *Proceedings of the Forty-first Annual Meeting of the State Historical Society of Wisconsin* (1894), pp. 79–112.

social control like the family, church, bench and bar, landholding and merchant elites, and the state.

In part, the emigrations to Oregon and California in the 1840s had their origin in the missionary travels of such men as Jason Lee, Marcus Whitman, and others in the previous decade. On September 12, 1836, the missionary doctor Marcus Whitman and his recent bride, Narcissa, together with the Reverend Henry Harmon Spaulding and his wife, Eliza, and William H. Gray, a layman, arrived at Fort Vancouver. Narcissa and Eliza were the first white women ever to cross the Rocky Mountains. Whitman subsequently established a mission at Waiilatpu, twenty-five miles above Fort Walla Walla, where he remained until November 29, 1847, when together with his wife and two children he was killed in an uprising of the Cayuse Indians. The Board of Missions of the Methodist Episcopal church brought the white man's "book of heaven" to the Nez Percé Indians in 1834, but it was not only for the purpose of Christianizing the savages that church groups turned to the West. The supposed immorality of cursing, hard-drinking, gambling western emigrants would be moderated, it was believed, by the influence of orthodox Protestantism; but perhaps a more important consideration was that if political power moved westward, then the moral order underpinning it could be maintained only if most men subscribed to the doctrines of organized religious groups.

In 1840 Joel P. Walker, his wife and children, and his wife's sister, set out for the Pacific, and perhaps he was the first homeseeker to go west to live with a family. They arrived at Sutter's Fort in October of 1841. Thereafter a steadily increasing number of emigrants started west each year, and it has been estimated that by 1865 more than 350,000 persons may have gone over the trails. Those who started out overland for Oregon and California in the early years were mostly young men, for they had the vigor and stamina needed to withstand the rigorous life on the trail. Even so, the ordeal aged some of them mightily. There were families with their children, of course, but in the beginning relatively few. The average age of the early western emigrant was about twenty-five while in the United States of the 1840s the average life expectancy was only about forty years. By 1850 this figure increased to forty-one years, but still, 25 percent of the newborn died before they were five years old.

The number of persons emigrating to Oregon between 1841 and

1852 has been estimated as between 18,000 and 19,000, distributed as follows: 1841–400; 1842–137; 1843–1,000; 1844–700; 1845–3,000; 1846–1,350; 1847–5,000; 1848–700; 1849–400; 1850–2,000; 1851–1,500; and 1852–2,500. These figures, to 1850, approximate those of Captain H. Stansbury of the U.S. Topographical Corps. It has been estimated that roughly 85 percent of the emigrants to California in 1849 were men; 10 percent were women, and 5 percent were children.

In St. Louis in the summer of 1840, the Western Colonization Society was organized; its objective was not Oregon, but California. Only a few prospective emigrants (gentlemen, roughnecks, schoolteachers, frontiersmen) showed up at the rendezvous in the spring of 1841, but this did not discourage its organizer, John Bidwell, from starting. There were fifteen wagons, four Red River carts, mules, horses, oxen (no cows), and a total of one hundred dollars in cash. Father Pierre-Jean DeSmet, a famous Jesuit missionary, with ten companions, including the famous mountain man Thomas "Broken Hand" Fitzpatrick as their guide, later joined the Bartleson-Bidwell group (Bartleson was elected captain of the train), thus making a total of eighty persons including five women and some children. Among the women were Nancy Kelsey and her baby; she became the first white woman to see the Great Salt Lake and to cross the Sierra Nevada Mountains. She was the second woman to come overland to California; Joel P. Walker's wife had preceded her by twenty days. Twenty-four persons from the Bartleson-Bidwell party split off to go to Oregon, but the remainder, including ten children, finally made it to John Marsh's ranch at Mt. Diablo, California, on November 4, 1841. It had been a hard journey.

In 1842 Dr. Elijah White, newly appointed Indian subagent for Oregon, went there with sixteen wagons. The leadership of the train was taken over on the way by Lansford W. Hastings, a man who later was to figure prominently in the history of the Overland Trail as the promulgator of the Hastings Cut-off. It was in the next year, however, that the great migration to Oregon occurred. While Joseph B. Chiles went to California with fourteen wagons and 100 emigrants, and Joseph Walker went there with 50 people (Walker's party consisted of 27 men between twenty and forty years old, with only 4 men over forty; 3 seventeen-year-old youths, 8 boys between three and thirteen, and only 8 women, 5 of whom were under thirty-six), more than 1,000 persons belonging to approximately 200 families left for Oregon in 120 wagons. The presence of these emigrants would have an important influence on the "Oregon question" and its resolution. The trek to the West became a continuous one, and although the numbers of emigrants fluctuated with the years, patterns for traveling along the Oregon and Overland trails became well established, so that by the early 1850s commercial tours to the Pacific were possible.

In 1844 the Stevens-Murphy party entered California; this was notable in that for the first time wagons were brought all the way from Missouri. In addition, one segment of this party opened the Truckee River Trail over the Sierra Nevadas.

Prior to the discovery of gold in California in 1848, the major thrust of the emigrant movement was to Oregon. It is estimated that in 1847 approximately 5,000 persons headed northwest, while only 1,000 or so went to California. In 1847 and 1848 the exodus of the Latter-day Saints across the plains brought several groups, the largest of which consisted of over 2,400 persons, to the region of the Great Salt Lake. In 1849 and thereafter thousands left for the gold fields of California to become rich, or for adventure, but not necessarily to settle down. They were mostly males, itinerant fortune hunters, including a scattering of gamblers, hired guns, thieves, confidence men, and adventurers. Family units going to California in 1849 were rare. This great western folk movement of the 1840s culminated forty years of exploration, and the power vacuum was rapidly filled by emigrating Americans, so that by the end of the Civil War the challenge of the West had been met and overcome. Much of the West had been explored by "mountain men," or free trappers. As the fur trade waned and died in the early 1840s, these colorful characters also passed into history. They were, however, responsible in some degree for opening the West to the pioneers. Their influence may not have been all good, and they probably weakened the Indians by debauching them with whiskey and infecting them with venereal disease and smallpox. But these early nineteenth-century explorations must not be underestimated as a prior necessity for the later westward movement. The annexation of Texas in 1845, of the Oregon region in 1846, and of the Spanish southwest, after the War of 1848, were a consequence of exploration and subsequent settlement.

Settlers following close on the heels of trappers and explorers needed some sort of organization, for out on the plains there were hostile Indians, murderers and renegades, fugitives from justice, and a thousand other real or imagined animate and inanimate dangers that a man and his family could not face alone. An emigrant needed friends, good friends that would stick by him through good times and bad, and companions on the long walk to the West Coast. A few tried to go it alone, for one reason or another, but it was a foolish thing to do, as bleached human bones mutely testified to the emigrants trudging by them. Most banded together in loosely knit groups collectively called "wagon trains." At jumping-off points along the river frontiers, the families and strangers joined up with others, hoping to have something in common besides the expectation of arriving alive and in good health at their destination. Sometimes a train of a dozen wagons or so consisted of families from the same state, or county, or town; other times people headed for the same destination banded together. But it has been noted time and again in trail journals that for a number of reasons few stayed in the same organization throughout the entire journey.

Early in the history of trans-Mississippi emigration, we find that Jesse Applegate's 1843 train consisted of 60 wagons divided into "fifteen divisions or platoons of four wagons each." It all sounded very military and tidy. Unfortunately, this over-elaborate organization disintegrated after only a few weeks of life on the plains. Guidebooks of the time advised that there should be not less than twenty wagons; others recommended that there be not more than 50 persons, preferably all men; still others suggested that a wagon train consist of no fewer than fifty men. It appears from the figures noted in various diaries that the average wagon train of the 1840s consisted of around fifteen to twenty wagons with perhaps 60 to 125 people. The Mormons had organized themselves minutely into units of tens, fifties, and hundreds. They generally remained tightly knit since all aboard were bound by a deep and common cause.

The emigrants began by attempting to formulate codes of conduct, or a "constitution," or rules, by which they could agree to govern themselves in an essentially lawless territory. Most of these, despite theoretical soundness and the occasional elegant language employed, fell apart in the face of stress caused by differences in personalities, fatal accidents, sickness, disillusionment, dishonesty, and many other all too human failings. There also was a gradual winnowing out by the speed at which individual units managed to cover the ground. If members of a wagon train were determined to stick together, its progress would have to be governed by the speed of the slowest member. This arrangement usually did not remain intact for more than a few weeks;

in the press of time and expediency, large trains, unwieldy to begin with, found themselves hopelessly strung out for miles along the trail, never again to come together. Smaller groups consisting of a few wagons were the essential close-knit unit crossing the plains rather than the large trains sometimes shown in some movies depicting journeys during this period. Sometimes several independently traveling trains would parallel one another for days, but then they gradually moved away from one another until out of sight.

There were "turnbacks." Families returned to the East because of loss of stock, which made it impossible for them to travel the long distance to the coast; or they became disillusioned with the hardships of the journey, or a death or serious illness marred the trip. Some were glad to be turning back and viewed their attempt as an ill-advised venture; others vowed they would try again as soon as they could.

When the emigrations to the West began in earnest in the 1840s, the era of the mountain man had passed. It was only natural, then, that some of these men, who knew the territory like the backs of their hands, would end up acting as guides for emigrant trains. Old Tom "Broken Hand" Fitzpatrick guided the Bartleson-Bidwell group in 1841, and others "took up the trade" as their beaver trapping careers ended.

The old guides were independent, self-reliant, and confident. They had trapped beaver, fought Indians, tracked in and out of totally unexplored territory. A few had taken squaw wives whom they elaborately fitted out with finery, and many had absorbed much Indian lore; indeed, their outward appearance was much like that of Indians. They were a daring, brave, and unintentionally heroic band of men. Survival under seemingly hopeless conditions was their strong point. An old trapper turned guide could do practically anything for himself. He could hunt buffalo, antelope, and birds, cure a horse, catch fish, escape from wolves, butcher game, find or cover a trail, cook, tan hides, mold bullets, make and mend his moccasins, dress furs, and usually drink more "rotgut" whiskey than was needed to pickle a buffalo. He was a good fighter too, whether with fists or knives, or rifle.

Jim Bridger, much in demand as a guide and scout, was a typical mountain man. He had been up the Missouri River with Ashley's expedition in 1822 when he was only eighteen years old. He soon became a leader among mountain men. He had discovered the Great Salt Lake, seen the wonders of Yellowstone, and was one of the first to cross South Pass. His knowledge of the West was detailed and accurate. He also was steeped in Indian lore and custom, and could even speak some of their languages. This was the kind of man any emigrant train would wish to have for a guide. Unfortunately, there were not enough mountain men like Tom Fitzpatrick, Joe Meek, Stephen Meek, and Jim Headspeath to go around. Necessity dictated that other and lesser men would have to be selected as train leaders and guides. Bidwell wrote that John Bartleson of Jackson County, Missouri, was selected to be captain of one train leaving for the Oregon Territory in 1841, and that "he was not the best man for the position, but we were given to understand that if he was not elected captain, he would not go, and he had seven or eight men with him, and we did not want the party diminished so he was chosen." He continued, "In five days after my arrival we were ready to start, but no one knew where to go, not even the Captain." It was not long thereafter that Bartleson was effectively displaced by Tom Fitzpatrick.

Leaders would be needed even if the trail were clearly marked from end to end. The leader, supposedly selected by a democratic process, was given authority, in the absence of sheriff or judge, to maintain order and oversee the progress of the journey. This was a large and heavy responsibility, and included seeing that the sick and injured were aided; that fair play was observed; and that injustices or misdeeds were punished. As we have seen, the leader could be deposed by popular vote if the wagon train members felt that he was not doing a good job. In view of all of his duties, the leader had to be a strong personality, willing to face a fight, and to make difficult decisions on the spot. A leader might or might not have been on the trail previously, and many wagon trains found themselves floundering, or leaderless, or following other more experienced hands. Some groups seemed to change leaders frequently, but others stuck with one for the entire journey. Psychological and physical pressures on leaders undoubtedly were great, and some cracked up under the strain. Most trail diaries are laconic on these occurrences, and one can only surmise the course of events ending up with the deposition of a leader. Did he stay with the train, rejected and insulted? Did he leave, either to join up with another group, or go back east? The fate of deposed leaders is not easy to discover.

Albert J. Nock wrote that "women can civilize a society, and men cannot." So it was that women were the glue that maintained the social fabric of the wagon train. Exactly what did women do for the five months or so on the trail? For one thing, they did *not* ride daintily across the plains, as is sometimes depicted. No, they either walked beside the wagons or rode in one—not too comfortable a ride at that. Leisure time did not exist for any women on the trail save the very young and very old. Women and children did most of the chores, generally under conditions more primitive than in their farm homes. The chores were continuous and arduous. Cramped in the dusty, squeaky, smelly, gradually decaying wagons, they cooked, mended, washed, cleaned, drove the team, tended the sick, took care of babies, stood by and encouraged their menfolk, and generally kept busy from dawn until after dusk.

Unmarried women were rare in the West, and since all eligible ones were quickly "asked for." James Johnson, writing in 1851, said that

as the immigrants [sic] spread themselves over the land, the unmarried females among them are picked up before they have proceeded far from the seaboard; and thus the scarcity of the sex increases the farther westward we go; and the value at which they are estimated by the men and by themselves increases, till, in the Far West, they attain a famine price, and there we have a paradise of women.

Any woman desiring a husband need only go West since in 1850 there were about 145 males to every 100 females in the frontier states and territories.

The wagon train wife soon lost her bloom—if she had not already lost it at some failing farm back east. She quickly found that wearing finery on the trail was folly, and plain common sense reduced her wardrobe to a basic dress or two. Some had started out with scarcely more than that. It was difficult or impossible to stay clean, let alone "pretty up" for either the menfolk or themselves. Alas! the wagon train wife generally was sweaty and somewhat smelly under her sunbonnet; red-eyed and horny-handed; frizzy-haired and much in need of skin and foot care, as the constant dust and burning sun of plains and desert did their slow, destructive work. Even young women aged a good deal on the trail, and personal appearance had to take second place to dire necessity, and indeed survival. The long and demanding hours, the back-breaking and onerous work, the worry and mental stress, and the sometimes severe physical conditions encountered on the five months walk, wrung youth and beauty and even the life from many a young girl—even those used to heavy work and hard times.

The modern image of the western pioneer women, and the reality, can easily be compared by looking at very early photographs taken of wagon train women. More often than not one sees them grim, wan, and unsmiling; a day's rest for them, except if sick and unavoidably bedridden in a jostling springless wagon, would be hard to come by, even after they reached their destination—if they ever did!

Years before the 1840 emigrations missionaries expressed interest in the West. It was believed that the evils brought to this vast territory should be balanced, or at least counteracted, by a Christian influence. The Indians were not receiving just treatment at the hands of the white man: this was well known, and propaganda had it that the Nez Percé had even requested that they be given the white man's "book of heaven." The appeal for Protestant missions among the Indians in the West was enticing, especially to the Methodists, and as early as the spring of 1834 the Reverend Jason Lee and his nephew Daniel Lee went forth to their calling. Thereafter a number of missionaries traveled the long road, and the names of Dr. Marcus Whitman, the Jesuit priest Father DeSmet, H. H. Spaulding, Elija White, Samuel Parker, Cushing Fells, and others, are well known for their work.

But not all men of the cloth were missionaries, and in the 1840s wagon trains included itinerant preachers, ordained ministers, evangelists, and priests. It was not enough, however, merely to preach the word of the Lord; a western missionary might also need to be, as a letter in the *Christian Advocate* of November 8, 1843, declared, " . . . carpenter and joiner, receiver and forwarder of goods, retail merchant, salmon trader and salter, boat and canoe maker, stone layer, blacksmith, farmer, cobbler, nurse, and physician." This about missionary duties in the Oregon Territory. There is no doubt that the Protestant missionaries to the Indians in the West helped accelerate the Oregon migrations, by both deeds and stories of life there.

Most of the emigrants were churchgoers or church members, likely belonging to some Protestant sect, and by 1849 dozens of Protestant preachers also were headed west. As Octavius T. Howe wrote: "No regiment in Cromwell's Ironsides ever went to battle with [more] Bibles or more religious instruction than the California companies of 1849."

At the start of the journey most members of the wagon train were inclined to keep the Sabbath and refrain both from travel and work. Later on, under the pressure of time and season, and the need to "beat the snow," seven days a week travel became necessary. Of course, resting one day each week could have benefits for bone-weary pioneers over and above purely religious considerations. If there were enough chores to be done, and a campsite was favorable, a wagon train would probably rest after some religious services on Sunday, but if there was no water in the vicinity, or if the weather was exceptionally fine, or the season pressing, the Sabbath would have to be kept on the road by each person in his own way. Furthermore, the weather, mechanical failures, and other unforeseen events often prevented a wagon train from traveling for six consecutive days; often people had to wait for a river to settle back to normal depth, or for some blacksmith work to be done, or for some other time-consuming task.

A preacher's duties on the trail were generally those of his brethren, except, of course, that he preached the Gospel when possible, especially on Sunday. He also said the appropriate words over bodies of the dead, comforted the bereaved, and occasionally married some pair who had discovered one another on the trail. The first trail marriage was reported by John Bidwell in 1841, who noted that one Isaac Helsey married one Miss Williams, the ceremony being performed by the Reverend Williams. Most ministers and preachers assumed that the communities yet to be founded would want to have the comforts of religion with them, and they were right.

Apparently few physicians hit the trail before the Gold Rush, and while there are a remarkable number of journals and diaries available, written by doctors during and after 1849, they are scarce before that time. In fact, only a few physicians or medically trained men headed for the trans-Mississippi West for some time. Doctors were few enough in the states and territories west of the Alleghenies and east of the Mississippi in the 1840s. The prospects for setting up practice and making a decent living off emigrant families were bleak during this decade. A doctor's career would flourish monetarily only in an urban area like Boston, New York, Philadelphia, or Baltimore, unless he cared to dispense his Dover's Powders, gamboge, dragon's blood, and purges and restoratives, together with such medical advice as he had gleaned from various sources, without charge, and perhaps after travelling wearying hours on poor roads to some patient's bedside. Frontier doctors were almost as poor as most of their patients, and the latter's record for prompt payment for services rendered was not good. Humanitarian feelings loomed large among doctors as they plodded along with a pioneer train. Except in dire circumstances, the doctor's nostrums and practices were suspect, and folk (self-administered) medical practice based on various systems flourished. In view of the limited medical education of many "doctors" of the day, this is not surprising.

In the cholera years the doctors labored mightily on the trail in treating the pathetic victims of the disease, but its cause and mode of transmission were unknown, and doctors themselves often fell victim to it. After 1849 many wagon trains made a point of having a doctor go along with them.

We will never know the West as the early emigrants saw and experienced it. That country is gone forever—too much along the way has changed, grossly or subtly. There is, however, one way in which we may yet obtain a fleeting glimpse of the people and country of that era, namely, by looking at paintings and drawings made by artists of the time who were there. The color, vitality, and drama of the period are depicted in many works which communicate the spirit of the old West. The buffalo and other animals, the plant life, the Indians, the hunters and trappers, the long lines of emigrant wagons, the "nooning" stops, the campfire activities, the towering mountains and broad rivers, all have been depicted by the artists of the 1800s. Many of these pictures accurately portray the West, and therefore serve as historical documents from which we may obtain some valid ideas. Other pictures, however, are highly romanticized, inaccurate, or totally imaginary, and critical observation and comparison with written descriptions often is needed to separate fact from fiction. Some artists never saw the scenes they painted, and they depended entirely on written descriptions, or the works of other artists, for inspiration. For example, Felix O.C. Darley illustrated Francis Parkman's *The Oregon Trail*, as well as James Fennimore Cooper's *The Prairie*, yet he never went west. In the same way Charles Wimar's *The Attack on the Emigrant Train*, painted in 1856, was executed in Düsseldorf, four years before he actually saw the plains with his own eyes! It should be added that later Wimar works on the West are based on firsthand observations, and some are eminently accurate as historical documents of the time.

Artists such as George Catlin, Alfred J. Miller, Karl Bodmer, and Gustavus Sohon did not travel with emigrant trains, but moved about in small, independent, wandering groups, civilian or military, sketching and painting as they went. The exigencies and hurly-burly of wagon train travel was not conducive to artistic production, and aside from crude sketches there was relatively little work done in wagon trains hurrying toward the West Coast. Every man had to pull his own weight, and a man who could hunt, fish, drive a team, repair a wagon, build a fire in a rainstorm, find a trail, safely ford a rushing stream, or locate a good campsite, was considered a much better comrade to pragmatic pioneers than someone who wandered off to sketch a landscape or birds or animals or friendly Indians.

Many of the emigrants did make sketches of topographical features of interest that they passed. Chief among these were Court House Rock, Chimney Rock, Scott's Bluffs, and Independence Rock. Some of these landmarks were mentioned in nearly all of the emigrant diaries in terms ranging from laconic to highly poetic. Court House Rock is a huge, squarish rock beside the Platte River Road, massive and solid in appearance. This dominating feature of the landscape is accompanied by a second, much less impressive, rock formation sometimes called the Jail or Jail House. W. Wadsworth wrote in *The National Wagon Road* (1858), a book about his 1852 journey:

Situated miles apart from any mountain range, this solitary rock, at a distance of six to eight miles, seems to rise up from the grassy plain, with sides nearly perpendicular, to the hight [sic] of nearly 400 feet . . . and the whole formation so completely resembling an ediface of vast dimension, as to appear more like a work of art than nature.

During the great emigration one could see hundreds of names carved and scrawled and printed on it—perhaps in the hope of some sort of immortality, but little over a hundred years have gone and the names have long since worn away.

The next natural wonder seen along the Platte River Road was Chimney Rock, a tall column rising about 325 feet. It stood along the trail like a long finger pointing upward, or like a tall chimney, and it never failed to elicit some sort of comment in an emigrant's diary. Now it has eroded considerably; doubtless in earlier times it was even more impressive than when the emigrants viewed it. From the sketches available one sees that there were considerable differences as to the actual appearance of the rock. It could be seen for miles away across the flat Nebraska plains, and was a landmark, a beacon, and a sign of progress.

Another scenic wonder, following Scott's Bluffs, itself a marvelous rise of hills above the North Platte River, was Independence Rock. The trail ran close enough by it so that hundreds of emigrants clambered over it to carve their names on it. Father DeSmet called it the "Register of the Desert." This rock was measured in 1870 and found to be 193 feet high at its north end, and 167 feet at its south end. It is 1,550 yards in circumference, and looks much like a giant Indian mound. It is said that the name "Independence" was derived from the fact that some fur trappers spent the Fourth of July in 1810 or 1811 camped by it—but there are other stories about how the name came about. The original party was supposed to have carved the word "independence" on the rock.

The terrible possibility of Indians attacking instantly arose in the minds of the farmer and merchant emigrants as soon as they saw a few hovering in the distance. All the rumors and tales of Indian torture and atrocity must have leaped to their minds as they frantically pulled out guns and rifles, which few knew how to fire properly. Bidwell reported that after his company became so excited upon seeing a white man who they thought had been surrounded and taken by Indians, they started to run at a full uncontrolled gallop—oxen, mules, horses, everything—until they were halted at a river bank. Here the cool head of Tom Fitzpatrick prevailed, and the wagons were arranged in a hollow square, all the by now exhausted animals being placed inside it. Eventually a few Indians did appear, but they proved friendly.

Along the upper reaches of the Platte roamed the Sioux and Cheyenne Indians, and from the Big Blue River crossing to the Platte forks lay the territory of the Pawnees. Sooner or later the emigrants would confront Indians. Sometimes the pioneers found themselves between rival war parties, Pawnee vs. Sioux or Cheyenne, but the Indians were not at that time very much interested in them, since they were fighting a war. Only rarely in the 1840s did the emigrants battle the Indians. Wild stories and rumors spread at the jumping-off points proved to be just that. The Indians were generally curious, playful, or threatening in turn, and they begged and robbed at various times. They desired horses, guns, whiskey, ammunition, blankets, and tobacco much more than the white man's scalp. But an isolated white man was taking a chance if going it alone in Indian territory.

The emigrants usually presented gifts to the Indians which, for the most part, placated them. In later years the Sioux and Cheyenne did become enemies of the white man; the 1850s and early 1860s were studded with incidents of massacre, burning, and looting. But even the primitive Digger tribe, around the Humboldt River, was more interested in things than in people. Nevertheless, emigrant trains had scouts and outriders, and posted guards around the circled wagons at night.

The sight of Indians on distant hills, or of smoke signals, was cause for an immediate alert among the men, and a scurrying of women and children into the shelter of the wagons. Often Indian war parties would pass the emigrants, and their colorful feathers and bodies, hide shields, lances, and bows were striking in their primitive beauty.

The vicinity of Fort Laramie became the site of numerous Indian villages during the early years of the emigration. Trade between the red man and white man flourished, and there were lively exchanges of crafted goods for manufactured goods, both useful and decorative. Sometimes the emigrants traded with the Indians they met on the trail. A few were clean and clothed to a respectable degree, whereas others were smelly and dirty, and practically naked—much to the consternation of some emigrants who promptly tried to clothe them. Occasionally an Indian village or tree burial site was passed. As trees became scarcer on the plains, the dead Indians were placed on raised burial platforms. These were often desecrated by passing travelers—who themselves were filled with indignation when one of their number died and had his own grave torn open. When trees were available, the Indians sometimes placed their dead in a buckskin basket kept in shape with wooden hoops, and the whole was fastened to the top branches. These were not disturbed as much as were the burial platforms, and, of course, many emigrants had a fear of disturbing the dead, or else felt that they should be allowed to remain in peace.

There were few black emigrants, so the problem of discrimination seldom, if ever, arose. The rich, distinguished by the excellence of their teams and gear, remained socially apart from the poor dirt farmers and clerks. To a large extent, however, trail life smoothed out the peaks and valleys of distinctions based on wealth, and the common goal of California or Oregon resulted in a fairly democratic system. There was some discrimination against the Mormons, as well as toward the southerners from the Ozarks and Tennessee. A few slaves were seen on the trail, but their eventual fate was not usually recorded.

So the people left civilization and hit the trail to a new land and a fresh start. Full of hope, full of plans, confident of the future, off they went to the wonderful West. We shall see how some of them fared.

2

BETWEEN HERE AND THERE

In 1823 General William Henry Ashley and his "enterprising young men" found the Arikara Indians hostile to the white man's continued intrusions and were thereby deflected from their goal of ascending the Missouri River to its source. This proved to be a stroke of good fortune for future emigrants, since the accumulated information from Ashley-Smith explorations of the land up to the headwaters of the Green and Platte rivers would prove an invaluable source of guidance to them. Of especial importance was the rediscovery of South Pass, the emigrants' gateway through the Rocky Mountains. It was first discovered in the 1812-13 expedition from St. Louis to Astoria on the Columbia River and back by three Kentucky hunters, Edward Robison, John Hoback, and Jacob Rezner, a man named Miller, and perhaps several others. A trail to the Pacific was not established, although a feasible crossing of the barrier mountains was indicated. When Jedediah Smith was killed in 1831, and Ashley died in 1838, a great deal of knowledge about western geography was lost. The expeditions led by Captain Benjamin Bonneville and others between 1832 and 1834 further mapped out what would eventually become the main road to California. Joseph Walker (1833) and Nathaniel Wyeth (1832-36) also contributed to the geographical knowledge of this area by their own travels.

An important point to note about the ultimate incursion of the white man into the West is that a "permanent Indian frontier" had been established by Congress as early as 1825, including *all* the land west of the Illinois, Missouri, and Arkansas rivers. This territory was to be forever an inviolate home for tribes driven out of their native lands in the Old Northwest and Southeast. These territories were now coveted by the white man, who also, by the way, found himself incompatible with the red man. By 1840, after numerous acts, treaties, statutes, and covenants, most of the Indians had been "resettled" beyond the frontier, where no pioneer would be interested in going, and where he was supposedly barred from going. It was common knowledge that the area which the red man had been so generously tendered was mostly a wasteland; it was, in fact, known as the Great American Desert. This desert covers approximately 900,000 square miles, or about 30 percent of the land area of the contiguous United States. Its influence extends over all or parts of North and South Dakota, Nebraska, Kansas, Oklahoma, Texas, New Mexico, Colorado, Wyoming, Montana, Idaho, Washington, Utah, Oregon, Nevada, California, and Arizona.

This notion of a wasteland derived from explorations led by Major Stephen H. Long in 1819–20 over the high plains to the Rocky Mountains, and from his description, published in 1823, of this semiarid country west of the 98th meridian and the mountains. It was believed to be a land totally useless for agricultural pursuits, or for anything else of interest to the white man. In the meantime, the land between the Alleghenies and the Mississippi River was being continually populated with fresh settlers from the East.

The words "unexplored desert" or "Great American Desert" soon were found in geography books and on maps depicting territory west of the Mississippi River. Insofar as it constituted a barrier to further advance by the white man, the frontier facing this so-called desert was easily and often breached as the pressures of civilization built up behind it and enticing tales about coastal paradises spread. Washington Irving, for example, described Bonneville's California in the following manner: "They came down upon the plains of New California, a fertile region extending along the coast, with magnificent forests, verdant savannas, and prairies that look like stately parks." Exactly what kind of lands did lie west of the Missouri River? The Missouri River itself was both a barrier and a highway. The scattered outposts of the American Fur Company, for example, were held together by steamboats traveling from St. Louis to the upper Missouri, and, of course, the settlements located here were the emigrants' jumping-off sites for the West.

The regions over which emigrants generally would have to travel comprised six physiographic areas, namely, central lowlands, interior plains, interior highlands, the Rocky Mountain system, intermountain plateaus, and the Pacific mountain system.

The interior plains consist of the central lowlands and Great Plains, the latter being a plateau that gradually rises from 1,000 to 2,000 feet on the eastern border with the central lowlands, to an altitude of 5,000 to 6,000 feet at the base of the Rocky Mountains. Emigrants traveling west of the Mississippi River thus crossed part of the central lowlands and the Great Plains before encountering the Rockies. The area of the plains was covered by a closed sod of perennial grasses that became more open to the south and northwest. Between the Rocky Mountain forests and the Sierra Nevada Mountains lies the desert. Here there are only two types of vegetation, the sagebush and the creosote bush. There is no water, wood, or grass, and only a few animals. In the south Rocky Mountains lies the Wyoming basin, and here emigrants were furnished with an easy passage, at South Pass. South Pass ("South" to distinguish it from northern passes in Montana) is situated at latitude 46° 26' in west-central Wyoming south of the Wind River Mountains. The ascent to this gap in the Rockies is very gradual, although the altitude at the summit of the pass is 7,489 feet. The pass is about twenty miles broad, and from the Sweetwater branch of the North Platte River leads to the Big Sandy branch of the Green River. The headwaters of the Snake and Green are not far from the pass. The country around the pass is completely open and timber is absent.

It has been pointed out that:[1]

When Lewis and Clark piloted the way into the far West, they crossed the Continental Divide between the Big Hole and the Bitter Root Valleys at an elevation of approximately nine thousand feet. The Astorians who went overland under Wilson Price Hunt made their way over Union Pass and the Teton Divide at about the same altitude. Both these parties had to struggle through rugged canyons and up precipitous slopes . . . . Had no easier way been found it is doubtful whether the rich regions beyond the Rockies would today be under the Stars and Stripes.

The intermountain plateaus are divided into three parts, the Colum-

---

[1]   H.R. Driggs, *Westward America*, p. 108

bia, the Colorado, and the basin and range region. The Columbia
Plateau includes the drainage basin of the Columbia River and the
Snake River. Some portions of the rivers run through very deep canyons. The Colorado Plateau is in the basin of the Colorado River at altitudes of from 6,000 to 10,000 feet. The basin and range region consists of a northern half, the Great Basin, while the southern part is related to the Sonoran district of Mexico, and to the Mexican highlands.

John C. Frémont wrote of his travels across the Great Basin:

The contents of the Great Basin are yet to be examined. That it is
peopled we know, but miserably and sparsely. From all that I heard
and saw, I should say that humanity here appeared in its lowest form,
and in its most elementary state . . . . The rabbit is the largest animal
known in the desert, its flesh affords a little meat . . . . The wild sage is
[the] only wood, and here it is of extraordinary size—sometimes a foot
in diameter, and six or eight feet high. It serves for fuel, for building
material, for shelter . . . . The whole idea of such a desert, and such a
people [the Digger Indians], is a novelty in our country, and excites
Asiatic, not American ideas.

The Great Basin is an ancient lake bed lying south of the Columbia Plateau. It extends for six hundred miles from the Wasatch Mountains of Utah to the Sierra Nevada and parts of southern Oregon and
eastern California. The basin is not a depression, however, and it lies
at an average elevation of 9,000 feet.

The Pacific mountain system consists of the Sierra-Cascade range
and the Pacific border. The Sierras are from 10,000 to 14,494 feet in
altitude, and the Cascade range is somewhat lower. The Columbia River, of course, flows through a gap in these mountains, and it was
through here that Lewis and Clark and later explorers went to the Pacific. There is no river gap through the Sierras, however, and various land
passages were used, the easiest one being Truckee Pass, discovered in
1844. After the emigrants crossed the Sierra-Cascade range, they entered either the California valley, the Willamette valley, or the Puget Sound
valley which separated the Sierra-Cascade range from the coastal mountains, namely, the Olympic, the Oregon, the Californian, and the Los
Angeles coastal ranges.

The mean ·average temperature of the northern plains in July is
around 70°F, with a maximum of around 110°F. The plateau region re-
ceives less than 20 inches of rainfall a year, and whereas the eastern side
of the plains has an annual fall of from 20 to 25 inches, the western side

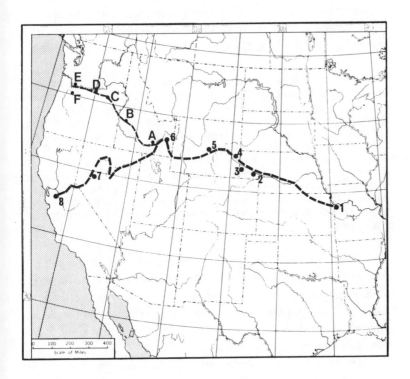

Fig. 2   The Overland and Oregon Trails in the 1840s.
Overland to California (1 through 8). (1) Westport
Landing; (2) Chimney Rock; (3) Scott's Bluffs;
(4) Fort Laramie; (5) Independence Rock; (6) Soda
Springs; (7) Carson Sink; (8) Mt. Diabolo. The Old
Oregon Trail (1 through 6 and A through F).
(A) Fort Hall; (B) Old Fort Boise; (C) Walla Walla;
(D) The Dalles; (E) Fort Vancouver; (F) Oregon
City.

averages less than 15 inches. In 1844 a great flood occurred in eastern Kansas and Nebraska. All the streams overflowed their banks, and even small creeks became impassable. The torrential daily downpour turned the prairie sod into mush and the wagon wheels sank into it up to the axles; consequently, all the trains were late in getting across the plains. Francis Parkman wrote in *The Oregon Trail:*

At last, towards evening, the old familiar black heads of thunder clouds rose fast upon the horizon, and the same deep muttering of distant thunder that had become the ordinary accompaniment of an afternoon journey began to roll hoarsely over the prairie. Only a few minutes elapsed before the whole sky was densely shrouded, and the prairie and some clusters of woods in front assumed a purple hue beneath the inky shadows. Suddenly from the densest fold of the cloud the flash leaped out, quivering again and again down to the edge of the prairie, and at the same instant came the sharp burst and the long rolling peal of the thunder . . . . It came upon us almost with the darkness of night, the trees, which were close at hand, were completely shrouded by the roaring torrents of rain.

Numerous diarists remarked on the intensity and force of thunderstorms on the prairie; lightning and hailstones were a constant threat to the emigrants. Although the emigrants did run into an occasional snow squall and frost, and even some freezing conditions on the plains, snow was generally not considered to be a problem except in the mountains, and then only late in the season.

On good days an ox-drawn wagon plodded along at a rate of two to three miles an hour, and the one-way walk from say, Independence, Missouri, to the Willamette valley of Oregon was one of over two thousand miles—something that gave a man pause to think before committing everything he had to the journey.

The valley of the Platte River was the central route of communication across the plains. In his *Overland Guide* H.B. Horn wrote of the Oregon Trail: " . . . the route designed by nature for the great thoroughfare to the Pacific. This was the road selected by nature's civil engineers, the buffalo, and the elk, for their Western travel. The Indians followed them in the same trail; then the traders, next the settlers came." It was almost a direct run from the jump-off points on the Missouri River to South Pass. The Platte River bottoms also provided the emigrants with wood for fuel, and with grass and water for the animals. It is ironic that this river was, and is, totally unnavigable, and even in high water seasons rarely achieves a depth of over five feet; no wonder then that it has been described as "a mile wide and an inch deep." But, together with the Kansas River, the Platte is one of the central feeders of the Missouri River. The 1,600-mile-long Platte is indeed about one mile wide at Grand Island, though readily fordable; but it is treacherous in many places, being peppered with potholes, sandbars, and quicksand.

Emigrants had to cross numerous creeks and streams, but in addition they faced major rivers such as the Kansas, the Big Blue, the lower Platte, the Laramie, the North Platte, the Green, the Snake, and the Bear. The Platte route traversed both sides of the river, and Council Bluffs Road on the northern side, sometimes called the Mormon Trail, originated near its mouth at the present-day Omaha–Council Bluffs area at places like Winter Quarters, Middle Ferry, and Trader's Point. The Mormons kept to the north side of the Platte River, and after passing Fort Bridger they headed for the Great Salt Lake through very difficult terrain along the Bear River divide and Weber Canyon. Emigrants starting from jump-off sites in the present St. Joseph-Kansas City area did not encounter the southern side of the Platte River for at least 200 miles.

With some minor variations, the trail for later emigrants led to the new Fort Kearney, the first sign of civilization since the Missouri River crossing. It was established in 1848, and was not, in fact, a fort but rather a crude housing arrangement for a small number of soldiers. E.A. Tompkins wrote about it in 1850 that

... [it] consist[s] of a kind of sod brick, or sods cut in the shape of bricks and heaped up after the form of a wall. Of such materials are the bodies of their buildings constructed and indeed the roof is made of the same material and placed on poles and brush. The floor is of solid earth. The quarters of the officers are a little more aristocratic being a fine two-story building. The object of this garrison is said to [be to] overawe the Indians of this region of the U.S. Territories and thus protect the emigrant.

Four hundred miles further was Fort Laramie, located at the juncture of Laramie Creek and the North Platte. It had been originally established in 1834 as an American fur trading post, but was taken over by the government and in 1849 housed several companies of soldiers. The fort itself consisted of a rectangular area, 40 by 120 feet, walled to a height of 10 feet with sun-dried bricks. There were limited stores of

Fig. 3   *Covered Wagons at Laramie Creek* by James F.
Wilkins. By permission of the State Historical
Society of Wisconsin.

Fig. 4   *Fording the Laramie Creek* by James F. Wilkins.
By permission of the State Historical Society of
Wisconsin.

sugar, tea, coffee, flour, and a few medicines available for purchase by
the emigrants at greatly inflated prices.

Then followed a 250-mile section from Fort Laramie to the Sweetwater River branch of the North Platte near South Pass. For the emigrants this was one of the most arduous and enervating parts of the
trail. Beyond the pass the road turned southwest to Fort Bridger, a trading post established by Jim Bridger in 1843 in the Green River valley.
Thence it turned northwest to Soda Springs, and from there to Fort
Hall on the Snake River plain. The Snake River is part of the Columbia
basin, and it is a river with a strong current. Its banks are composed of
volcanic rock, and numerous rapids make it unnavigable until after its
juncture with the Clearwater River. Near the juncture of the Snake and
Salmon rivers, the former passes through a canyon over three thousand
feet deep. Continuing along, the trail finally traversed the Grande Ronde
valley and crossed over the Blue Mountains to Walla Walla, descending
the Columbia River to Fort Vancouver and the Willamette valley.

In 1845 Samuel K. Barlow established yet another important segment of the route to the Pacific. Barlow's Road ran from The Dalles
on the Columbia River, southward on the Deschutes River, and then
west between Mount Hood and Mount Wilson, and then down the Sandy
River to Oregon City.

The route to California, the Overland Trail, branched off from
the Oregon Trail at the Raft River, approximately 150 miles beyond
South Pass, and in many aspects was more varied and difficult, the chief
obstacles being deserts and the Sierra Nevada Mountains. The California Trail ran from Fort Smith on the Arkansas River to Santa Fe, but
the Overland Trail and California Trail are often used to mean the same
thing, i.e., the northern route to California. The Overland Trail generally followed the Humboldt River to a point where, after a desert crossing, the Carson River was met. The Humboldt rises in the mountains
west of the Great Salt Lake from two rivers which unite after some fifty
miles. It is a narrow stream, without affluents, and it has low shores
lined with bulrushes and saline encrustations. It terminates in a sink
fifty miles from the base of the Sierra Nevadas, and for three hundred
miles was the sole source of water, grass, and wood. In the dry season
it varies from two to six feet in depth, and it passes through an arid,
sandy, grassless, woodless plain. The valley of the Humboldt, however,
was covered with edible grasses for animals, and marked by a line of cottonwood and willow trees. The Carson and Walker rivers are each nearly

one hundred miles long, arising from the Sierra Nevadas, and ending in lakes bearing their name. Thereafter California was entered either by Carson Pass or by the Truckee River and Pass, or the Lawson Route over the Sierra Nevadas.

Numerous shortcuts, or "cut-offs," were tried and recommended as more emigrants moved west, and some, such as the Hastings Cut-off, led to the disastrous predicament of the Donner Party in 1846. At South Pass, for example, instead of following the trail to Fort Bridger and Fort Hall, emigrants could travel directly west, via the Greenwood, or Sublette Cut-off, and arrive on the main road at the upper Bear River. Of course there was very difficult desert country to traverse. In 1849 Hudspeth's Cut-off was opened; it ran southwest for 120 miles, meeting the upper Raft River at a point where it joined the Overland Trail from Fort Hall. Once emigrants arrived on the mysterious and sullen Humboldt River, the great majority of them continued down it, but some left at the Great Bend and struggled westward across the desert and over the Sierra Nevadas. By the end of 1844 the trail to California was an accepted fact, but both trails were alive with emigrants even beyond 1869 when the Golden Spike marked the completion of the first transcontinental railroad.

Hiram M. Chittenden, looking back on the greatest of nineteenth-century folk migrations, characterized the development of the Oregon Trail when he wrote:

This wonderful highway was in its broadest sense a national road, although not surveyed or built under the auspices of the government. It was the route of national movement—the migration of a people seeking to avail itself of opportunities which have come but rarely in the history of the world, and which will never come again. . . . As a highway of travel the Oregon Trail is the most remarkable known to history. Consider the fact that it originated with the spontaneous use of travelers; that no transit ever located a foot of it; that no level established its grade; that no engineer sought out its fords or built any bridges or surveyed the mountain passes, that there was no grading to speak of nor any attempt at metalling the roadbed; and the general good quality of this two thousand miles of highway will seem most extraordinary.

After the Oregon Boundary Settlement of 1845, and once the Mexican War ceased in 1848, the West became an American entity—a country of vast dimensions and rugged terrain, yet with many desirable places to move into and develop. It has been pointed out that the decades of exploration prior to 1845 cannot be characterized solely in economic terms, and that, in fact, there was a clash of cultures on a grand scale, both in the wilderness (white man vs. red man) and back in civilization (American vs. Spanish and English). We will now follow the emigrants as they head out to this new country, and especially note how they equipped and supplied themselves with what they supposed were to be all the necessities for their great adventure.

3

BAGS AND BAGGAGE

The emigrants set out on their western trek in various states of preparation. Some were elaborately overequipped, but with many of the wrong things, and the road soon became littered with all sorts of fondly remembered but useless artifacts from the life back home. Carved chests of drawers, bookcases and books, picture frames, pianos, iron stoves, tools, utensils, clothing, and a thousand other imagined necessities were cast aside in the grim requirement of lightening the burden on exhausted animals, weakening wagons, and men. A few emigrants were poorly furnished, having sold or lost nearly everything of value; indeed, this was their reason for setting out for a fresh start. Some began their journey in almost pure ignorance, and they approached it as if going off on an afternoon's picnic outing. Many had never camped out before, and others imagined pleasant sojourns such as they had experienced in eastern forests. There was advice to be had, indeed, too much, and oftentimes false or flatly contradictory. Gratuitous tips were given by persons who never had made a complete journey to Oregon or California, and likely as not, they were based on tales, rumors, and hearsay.

All kinds of wheeled, animal-drawn vehicles were used, but the covered wagon, or prairie schooner, was one of the most common sights on the trail. Peter H. Burnett[1] gave the following advice about wagons

---

[1] Letter of Peter H. Burnett to James G. Bennett, received January 6, 1845. "Letters of Peter H. Burnett," *Oregon Historical Quarterly* 2 (1902): 398–426.

in a letter written in 1844:

The wagons for this trip should be two-horse wagons, plain yankee beds, the running gear made of good materials, and fine workmanship, with falling tongues; and all in a good state of repair. A few extra iron bolts, linchpins, skeins, paint bands for the axle, one cold chisel, a few pounds of wrought nails, assorted, several papers of cut tacks, and some hoop iron, and a punch for making holes in the hoop iron, a few chisels, hand-saw, drawing knife, axes, and tools generally; it would be well to bring, especially, augers, as they might be needed on the way for repairing. All light tools that a man has, that do not weigh too much, he ought to bring. Falling tongues are greatly superior to others, though both will do. You frequently pass across hollows that have very steep, but short banks, where falling tongues are preferable, and there are no trees on the way to break them. The wagon sheets should be double and not painted, as that makes them break. The wagon should be well made and strong, and it is best to have sideboards, and have the upper edge of the wagon body beveled outward, so that the water running down the wagon sheets, when it strikes the body may run down on the outside; and it is well to have the bottom of the wagon beveled in the same way; that the water may not run inside the wagon. Having your wagons well prepared, they are as secure, almost, as a house. Tents and wagon sheets are best made of heavy brown cotton drilling, and will last well all the way. They should be well fastened down. When you reach the mountains, if your wagons are not well made of seasoned timber, the tires become loose. [Wagons had to be constructed of well-seasoned wood to avoid shrinking of wheels and loosening of the iron tires in hot and dry regions. Osage orange, or white oak, generally was preferred for wagon building, however, Shively's *Guide* recommended that maple be used.] Loose tires were easily repaired by taking the hoop iron, taking the nails out of the tire, and driving the hoop iron under the tire and between it and the felloes, the tire you punch, and make holes through the hoop iron and drive in your nails, and all will be tight. . . . Beware of heavy wagons, as they break down your teams for no purpose, and you will not need them. Light wagons will carry all you want, and there is nothing to break them down, no logs, no stumps, no rock, until you get more than half way, when your load is so reduced that there is no danger.

Joel Palmer suggested that the iron tires should not be less than 1¾ inches wide, and that 2- to 3- inch widths were desirable; furthermore, they should be fastened with bolts rather than nails. Palmer believed that ". . . the Mormon-fashioned wagon was best, because they [sic] were usually made straight with 16 inch sideboards, and had a projection of four inches width and then another sideboard of 12 inches, between which the cover bows were set."

A covered wagon might be as long as a bedroom, and sufficiently wide for a person to lie full-length across it. The canvas or Osnaburg (a kind of coarse linen cloth first manufactured in Osnaburg, Germany) sheeting that served as a cover was stretched over the wagon, supported by oak bows. Flax or tow sheeting prevented the rain from seeping through except in the most severe and driving rainstorms, and a double thickness was even more desirable. The front and rear of the wagon were left open, but could be securely closed by means of curtains that buttoned on the side. No space was wasted, and even the underside was used to hang or lash lanterns, buckets, churns, farming tools, and water kegs. Inside the wagon baskets, iron pots and pans, clothing and other paraphernalia hung from the bows, and patch pockets for holding various articles were sewn in everywhere. Beds were arranged in the wagon bottom and chores were done on them or around them as space allowed. The cookstove, if one was carried along, usually was placed at the rear of the wagon where it could be easily pushed out on a small shelf. One or more water kegs were lashed to the rear axle and a "tar bucket" which contained tar or resin mixed with an equal amount of tallow was also hung there. The contents of the latter were brushed on axles to reduce wheel screeching when it became unbearable. A privy or slop bucket was arranged in the rear of one of the wagons, although the rule of "gents-to-the-left, ladies-to-the-right" or vice versa, also was employed on the trail. (See chapter 5.) Someplace in a well-supplied wagon one could also expect to find extra wagon parts, as well as a spade, axe, hatchet, lanterns, an adz, a hammer or maul, and tools that were imagined to be essential, or too valuable to be left behind, or unavailable in Oregon or California. Generally there was room for only two adults to sleep in the wagon, and tents had to be brought along for additional members of the party, if it was a single-wagon journey. During good weather some men slept under their wagons.

Most of the vehicles used on the Santa Fe Trail were Murphy wagons, manufactured in St. Louis by a company of that name, although popular wagons also were made by Schuttler, Bain, and Moline. They were high, awkward vehicles, 3 feet wide and up to 16 feet long, with rear wheels 5 feet tall circled by iron tires 4 inches wide, obviously constructed for hauling heavy loads of freight and commercial goods. The Conestoga wagon, developed in Pennsylvania in the

1750s, was designed for transporting loads of three to four tons, but it was not used much on the trail because of its great bulk, weight, and concave bottom. The prairie schooner, by contrast, was generally a converted flat-bed farm wagon covered with canvas draped over wooden bows, and much lighter and more fragile than the Conestoga type.

A prairie schooner did not, unfortunately, "sail" over the prairies, and in fact, it was a difficult and intractable machine, being equipped with neither brakes nor springs. It was a muscle-pulling, back-breaking job to push it out of the sloughs or up steep inclines. Its ride was bumpy and teeth-rattling as it crunched over rough, hard, uneven ground; it was draughty and cold; it was dusty and hard to keep clean; it was hot; it smelled of animal dung and urine; it got wet inside when it rained heavily for a time; it squeaked, groaned, flapped, rattled, rocked, swayed, and dipped. It was a dangerous job for teamsters and drivers to handle, and anyone suffering from a nagging toothache, or headache, or sprained back, or bad stomach, to mention only a few common ailments of emigrants, got little, if any, comfort or rest in a prairie schooner while it was plowing over the plains. Even when stationary, these wagons were little more than wheeled hovels.

If the wagon bed was waterproofed, it could be made into a sort of boat by removing bolts and couplings attached to the running gear and removing the wheels. Fording swift running streams or rivers with a farm wagon was a problem few emigrants had previously encountered. A train of fifty to one hundred wagons might start off in a group or company; sometimes they stuck together, but often they split up in various ways as they proceeded down the trail. Accidents, arguments, long delays at ferries and fording places, and the slow pace of some, gradually stretched them out so as even to lose contact with one another.

The wheeled vehicles were pulled by oxen, mules, or horses. An emigrant could get plenty of suggestions as to what was best for him in this regard. Selecting animals was a matter not to be taken lightly, for indeed, a family's lives ultimately depended on the well-being of their animals, and in some cases, after months of hard service, they had to be sacrificed for food, or because they were completely worn out and useless for further work. The trail was littered with the skeletons and rotting carcasses of thousands of animals who died in faithful duty to their masters, and although some families became very much attached to their animals, others were too exhausted or indifferent to care, and they let the beasts die where they faltered and stumbled on the trail.

Good mules cost about one hundred dollars each in the early 1840s, but they withstood the heat well, and were more sure-footed and traveled faster (twenty to forty miles per day on good ground) than oxen. They were high-strung and dangerous, and many an unwary emigrant purchased half-broken or even completely wild animals. A farmer whose sole experience was driving a buggy pulled by a placid old mare was in for a shocking surprise when he first tried to work with untrained mules. Over the long haul oxen were more reliable and durable, especially on rough or muddy trails, but they could not easily get at the short spring grass, as mules or horses could, and thus might hold up a caravan anxiously straining to start west. Oxen raised in Illinois or Missouri were preferable to those from Indiana or Ohio because they had been accustomed to prairie grass—their only food while on the trail. Three well-ordered yoke of oxen from four to seven years old were better than six horses, except with very light wagons. Oxen were cheaper than mules (about fifty dollars each), and although slow (two to three miles per hour, or twelve to fifteen miles per day on good ground), they had the advantages of a placid disposition, strength, and edibility in emergency. Six average size oxen (three yoke) could be expected to pull a load of around 2¼ tons—the allowance of four adults. Furthermore, oxen were not especially desired by the Indians; they could be allowed to graze out at night without staking, and stampedes among them were rare. Each horse and mule should have been provided with a half-inch lariat forty feet in length, for staking out at night, but these items were sometimes forgotten or lost, and the animals then were kept on an uncomfortably short tether. A few cows were useful to take along as sources of milk and butter, or even for emergency harnessing if necessary.

A number of ingenious methods were used for estimating the daily mileage covered. For example, when the Mormons went west in 1847, Brigham Young asked Orson Pratt to devise a "roadmeter," and he did so in a remarkably short time. He wrote:

Let a wagon wheel be of such a circumference that 360 revolutions make one mile. . . . Let this wheel act upon a screw, in such a manner that six revolutions of the wagon wheel shall give the screw one revolution. Let the threads of this screw act upon a wheel of sixty cogs, which will evidently perform one revolution per mile. Let this wheel of sixty cogs be the head of another screw, acting upon another wheel of thirty cogs. It is evident that in the movements of the second wheel, each cog will represent one mile. Now, if the cogs were numbered from 0 to 30, the number of miles traveled will be indicated during every part of the day.

All sorts of advice also were available regarding what emigrants should and should not carry with them in the way of food and other supplies. Independence, Missouri, for example, had an unlimited abundance of supplies, and the bustling town boasted saddle and harness makers, mule markets, tinsmith and blacksmith shops, wheelwrights, hatters, furriers, gunsmiths, and clothing establishments; it even had a flour mill and a rope mill.

Some experts advised emigrants to take 200 pounds of flour for each person over ten years old, and 100 pounds for each person over three and under ten; 15 pounds of coffee and 15 pounds of sugar for each person; 100 pounds of bacon for each person over ten years old and 50 pounds for all those over three and under ten. Bacon was packed in strong sacks, 100 pounds to the sack. To prevent the fat from melting in the heat of the plains, it was stored in boxes surrounded by bran. Flour was kept in double canvas sacks, and sugar in India rubber bags. Finally, each mess was advised to take 50 pounds of salt, 50 pounds of rice, 5 pounds of pepper, 50 pounds of dried apples and peaches. In 1846 superfine flour sold for $2.00 to $2.25 per 100 pounds; beans were $1.50 a bushel, and coffee and sugar were $0.10 per pound, while tea ranged between $0.75 and $1.50 per pound.

Diets could be supplemented with meat from buffalo, antelope, squirrels, game birds, and the like, as well as with fish and berries, but it was not considered wise to count too heavily on these as a regular source of food. Many emigrants carried along such relatively stable items as corn meal, hard cheese, crackers, molasses, pickled and smoked meat, hardtack, yeast, saleratus, maple sugar, vinegar, whiskey, and brandy. Food supplies were generally estimated on the basis of starting out in late April or early May for a 3½ to 5 months journey—and individual needs and choices varied widely. Without doubt, sowbelly, biscuits, and coffee were the staples of the trail.

Some emigrants carried along "cold flour," or penole. It was a preparation developed in the Spanish southwest country, consisting of parched corn pounded fine and mixed with sugar or molasses and cinnamon. When this was combined with water and stirred, it made a satisfactory meal. It was estimated that half a bushel of penole would allow a man to subsist for at least thirty days. It was an especially useful food since it required no fire to cook it, and occupied little space in proportion to its weight.

Dried vegetables were prepared by pressing out the juice and placing the remaining material in an oven until it was completely dehydrated. It was rock-hard, but when reconstituted with boiling water served as an antiscorbutic. This material kept very well if protected from dampness. Canned foods were not generally available until the 1850s.

Pemmican was used by explorers and mountain men, but not very much by the emigrants. It was made by pounding dried jerky into powder and filling containers about half full of it. (Dried jerky was prepared as follows: A smudge fire was built and maintained under an elevated framework upon whose top surface thin strips of buffalo meat were placed. After two days the meat was smoke-cured and would remain preserved until eaten if kept dry.) Melted buffalo fat was then mixed with the powdered jerky, in a proportion considered right, and then it was set aside to harden. It was a very rich source of nutriment for a man with nothing else to eat.

China, if taken, was packed in flour barrels, but meals were generally eaten off cheap tinware. Cooking utensils and kettles were made of iron, and capable of being used over open fires. A Dutch oven, for baking, consisted of a shallow iron kettle with a rimmed cover for holding hot coals. A spider, also a commonly used piece of cooking equipment, was essentially a long-handled skillet with legs, and, therefore, it could be set over a fire. There was no wood on the plains, and any tree that had grown there was quickly chopped down to be used as fuel. Emigrants would travel hundreds of miles without seeing a single tree. "Buffalo chips" became the wood of the prairie, and these light mats of dried buffalo dung could be employed much like hickory coals. The children and women of emigrant families were responsible for gathering enough chips every day to ensure a fire for a hot meal when they stopped to camp for the night. Water was dipped from streams or pools, and sometimes the "wiggletails" had to be strained out before it could be drunk. Finding a source of water was an important part of each day's march.

Although all emigrants probably had some "store bought" items of clothing, strong and cheap, almost every kind of homespun and homemade garment was in evidence. Some early pioneers copied their style from the Indians, and buckskin pantaloons and fringed deerskin hunting shirts, open at the neck, were often seen. Linsey-woolsey, a coarse fabric woven from linen warp and a wool yarn filling, and calico, were used for making outer clothing such as shirts and dresses, as well as underwear. Clothing was handed down as necessary, and often it was too large on some children (so they could grow into it) and too small on others (because they had grown out of it). Patches, often not matching the clothing covered, were commonly seen adorning adults' clothing as well as children's. Broad-brimmed felt hats for men, and poke bonnets for women, helped protect the emigrants from glare and sunburn. Rough woolen sack coats with large pockets were worn by men, and they are commonly depicted as wearing their tight trousers stuffed into high boots. Men are also described as wearing brown woolen jackets, linen shirts, bright-colored neckerchiefs, broad leather belts, and ten-gallon hats. Before flax was grown, hair from cattle, buffalo wool, and sometimes wild nettle lint were spun and woven into cloth, which was then cut and sewn into shirts, dresses, trousers, and other articles. Wool, when available, was dyed with a concoction made from walnut or butternut bark; this is the reason why most pioneer clothing was brown. Children generally went without shoes in the summer, but aside from boots, moccasins made from deerskin were popular. Often moccasins were made large so that they could be stuffed with deer hair or dried leaves to keep the feet dry. Members of families using ox-drawn wagons walked nearly all the time unless too young, or ill, or injured.

Taken in the wagons were blankets, sheets, quilts, coverlets, and pillows—but no beds. Gutta-percha, oilskins, or painted canvas sheets were used for protection against dampness. Coarse linen thread for mending, together with beeswax, buttons, and large needles were taken along for the numerous mending chores likely to be met.

The medicine chest might contain any number of remedies in the form of elixirs, tonics, salves, balms, unctions, and ointments, together with "physiking pills," laudanum, calomel, essence of peppermint, castor oil, and a few patent medicines. Laudanum was a tincture of opium, and calomel a powder or pill preparation containing mercurous chloride; the former was used for relief of pain and the latter as a purgative.

Many men were walking arsenals, apparently following Shiveley's *Guide* which advised, "Go well armed, and never let your guns get out of order; and, to avoid accident, carry them without caps." Martin wrote that each man ought to be armed with a heavy shotgun or good rifle, and be supplied with five pounds of powder and twelve pounds of lead or fifteen pounds of shot. Knives and daggers of all sorts were carried for protection, for skinning animals, and for doing mechanical chores.

Violins, flutes, banjoes, and jew's-harps are recorded as being among the musical instruments taken along for amusement or solace on the trail. Although books were packed in some wagons at the start of the journey, the road eventually became a veritable lending library, as the necessity for lightening the load became inevitable. In the end, most books, except the Bible, and maybe one of the several popular home medical advisors, were discarded.

The initial cash outlay for gear and food in 1849 was estimated to be around $700. One list proposed costs as follows: "Wagon, $85.00; 3 sett of harness, $8.00 each, $24.00; mules, $75.00 each, $450.00 for 6; wagon cover painted with 2 coats, $8.00; total $567.00." Flour, bacon, coffee, sugar, lard, beans, peaches and apples, salt, pepper, and saleratus for four people came to $83.18; cooking utensils including tin plates, spoons, coffeepot, camp kettle, knives, and extras, $20.00; making the cost about $670.78, or $167.69 per person! Deducting the value of the wagon, teams, etc., at journey's end, estimated at $450.00, the final expenditure was calculated to be $55.19 per person.

Thus equipped, or over- or underequipped, the emigrants crossed the broad Missouri River and hopefully began their long walks to the green and golden lands of Oregon and California.

4

DOCTORS AND DOCTORING
IN THE FORTIES

The high death rate (about 3 percent per annum) of Americans in the 1840s was only incidentally affected by the fact that doctors of this time were poorly trained. One American doctor asserted that "... the boy to go into medicine was the son too weak or too lazy for farm or shop, too stupid for the bar, and too immoral for the pulpit." Although most states had laws on their statute books regarding licensing, by 1845 only three had made any serious effort to enforce them. A man could be fined for practicing medicine without a license, and even denied his fees, but since medical examinations were informalities, and easily obtained from a state board appointed by a local medical society, almost anyone could, with but little effort, practice medicine legally.

The West badly needed doctors, but the few medical schools in the eastern states could not supply them, so it seemed expedient that new schools would have to be founded. This was a fairly simple matter. As Sigerist[1] observed:

Medical schools shot up like mushrooms after a night rain. There were hardly any governmental regulations. Whenever a few doctors gathered together, they could found a school, get a charter, call themselves professors, give medical instruction in some rented building, deal out diplomas, and pocket the tuition fees. It was a good business. . . .

---

[1]   H.E. Sigerist, *American Medicine* (New York: W.W. Norton, 1934), p. 132.

Under these circumstances, the education of future doctors was minimal. There were few books and supplies, no cadavers for instructional purposes, and no laboratory facilities worth mentioning. The students were exposed largely to theory and only bits and snippets of practical medicine, and after two years (the second usually being merely a repetition of the first) the new "doctor" went forth to "treat" his patients. It is difficult to give an exact figure on the number of medical schools in existence, because many of their doors were closed soon after their establishment; but between 1810 and 1840 twenty-six new schools were founded, and from 1840 to 1876 forty-seven more were started. It is little wonder, then, that poor doctors were the rule, and consequently, the prestige of an average practitioner was low.

Some doctors had never attended a university, but learned their medicine by attaching themselves to a practitioner or "preceptor." After "living in" for a few years, during which the young apprentice cleaned the doctor's office, did the chores, rolled pills, read the available medical books, and observed what he could, he was "certified" by his master that he, too, at the ripe age of nineteen or twenty, was now competent to practice medicine and be called "doctor." The lack of adequate training and standards, the diagnostic blunders, and incessant arguments and contradictory advice over treatments, and an overweening interest in collecting fees, all militated in raising grave doubts in the layman's mind about the wisdom of calling in a doctor during a time of illness. Probably most of the sick never called a doctor in, but rather, treated themselves or were ministered to by some member of the family, usually the mother, or a neighbor, with a battery of home remedies and potent concoctions.

During the early part of the nineteenth century, various medical sects arose, among them homeopaths, hydropaths, Indian doctors, mesmerists, Thomsonians, chrono-thermalists, uroscopians, and faith doctors. These sects claimed the right to practice medicine and confer licences in the same way that the "legitimate" medical societies did. Medical anarchy now was a fact, and anyone denied a license from a state board to practice legitimate medicine could always get one from some group or other—quacks and charlatans flourished, and the patient was indeed the victim. Small wonder indeed that doctors were not trusted.

Samuel C.F. Hahnemann's system of homeopathy was based on the theory that a disease was best treated by using very small doses of a drug that produced the symptoms of the disease. The Thomsonian system was invented and developed by Samuel Thomson, a New Hampshire farmer; it was based upon the theory that the "life force" is an electrical fluid which appears in the body as heat. If one increased the body's heat, one increased the life force; consequently, patients were treated in a steam bath, or given sweat-inducing herbs, numerous enemas to purge them of poison, *Lobelia* to induce vomiting, and combinations of six medicines concocted from a selection of seventy herbs to cure them.

Although Thomsonian medicine and homeopathic medicine may not have effected many cures, in spite of the claims made for these systems by advocates, they were relatively benign in contrast to the brutal and excessive bloodletting, purging, blistering, mercurial poisoning, and surgical butchery practiced by many regular doctors of the time. The removal of undesirable body humors was facilitated by bleeding. Sixteen to twenty-four ounces of blood were drawn from a blood vessel by means of a sharp lancet; or by "cupping," that is, making a number of perforations in the skin and applying a heated bleeding cup, which, upon cooling, formed a vacuum, thus drawing out the blood; or by applying leeches directly to the skin. Purging was induced by use of cathartics and emetics including castor oil, calomel, ipecacuanha, opium, tartar emetic, calcined magnesia, and cream of tartar. After the bad humors thus had been driven out, the body was rebuilt by means of various "tonics" and "restoratives."

In general, medical practice in the forties was primitive and sometimes dangerous; surgical operations, for example, were always attended by the constant threat of shock and infection. Chloroform had been discovered in 1831, and Dr. Crawford Long had used ether for an operation in 1842, but the only generally used painkillers were laudanum (opium), morphine, and whiskey. Sir Humphrey Davy wrote in 1799 that nitrous oxide (laughing gas) " . . . seems capable of destroying physical pain, it may probably be used with advantage in surgical operations in which no great diffusion of blood takes place." Unfortunately, it was left unused except as a circus curiosity until 1844. The work of Louis Pasteur and Robert Koch still lay in the future, and many operations were attended by surgeon-caused bacterial infections.

As to infectious diseases, communities of the newly settled frontier country were periodically ravaged by epidemics of typhoid fever, pneumonia, erysipelas, diphtheria, measles, whooping cough, dysentery, mumps, and a host of other ill-defined ailments. Cholera periodically swept the land, the first epidemic occurring in 1832-34. Ague was very common, and the malaria-like diseases, or autumnal fevers, were also. Daniel Drake, in his monumental study of the diseases in the interior valley, classified febrile fevers as including: intermittent fever, simple, and inflammatory; malignant intermittent fever; remittent fever; malignant remittent fever; and protracted, congestive, miasmatic, marsh, chill, malarial, ague, fever and ague, dumb ague, relapsing, and vernal intermittent fevers.

There were, of course, treatments and "cures" for all these illnesses, and the citizens of villages, hamlets, and towns in trans-Allegheny United States often practiced their own unique and often spectacular brands of folk medicine. In the minds of pioneer settlers, sickness could be due to many causes, including the weather, poor eating and drinking habits, "sickly" dispositions, and mysterious workings not mentioned aloud. The list of "ailments" mentioned in the 1830s, for example, is astounding; one finds rickets, cancers, sciatica, weak lungs, asthma, nervous tremors, sick stomach, croup, pleurisy, dyspepsia, worms, rheumatism, fits, itch, lumbago, palsy, cramps, palpitation of the heart, liver complaint, biliousness, dropsy, and green sickness. Between 1820 and 1870 the chief endemic infections were enteritic in the summer and respiratory in the winter. By 1850 the chief cause of death was pulmonary tuberculosis, although smallpox remained as one of the chief causes of death in cities as late as 1860. Cholera epidemics scourged the nation in the 1830s, 1840s, and 1860s.

Many "cures" were as formidable as the ailments themselves, and in the common household remedy books, almanacs, and newspapers, herbs and herbal concoctions were frequently advised. The influence of Indian medical practices was plain. The treatments employed for illness occurring on the trail were largely based on folk remedies and traditional, primitive, home resources.

Some of these recipes have survived in the backwaters of modern civilization, and even today, "nanny tea," a hot-water extract of sheep dung, is used for "bringing out" measles. Persons suffering from "fever" were given concoctions made from sassafras, dogwood or willow; cold sufferers might be administered a mixture of white vinegar in which sugar candy, raisins, licorice, and flaxseed were included. "Bitters" was a special favorite among home remedies, being prescribed for cholera, croup, whooping cough, phthisis, colds, and

Fig. 5   Medicine chest. Common medicines carried in a
traveling doctor's kit are seen, including calomel,
camphor, morphine, and belladonna. Courtesy of
the Armed Forces Institute of Pathology,
Washington, D. C.

Fig. 6   Amputating instruments. This is a rather simple
           set, used when traveling. The contents were: one
           Capital saw, one Metarpal saw, two Capital
           knives, one Catlin knife, one pair of Liston's
           artery forceps. Other elaborate sets were
           maintained in hospital surgeries. Courtesy of
           the Armed Forces Institute of Pathology,
           Washington, D. C.

jaundice. Recipes for preparing bitters were plentiful and called for stewed or crushed wild cherry, dewberry, yellow poplar, or sarsaparilla combined with whiskey, brandy, cider, and sumac or bitter roots. All kinds of roots, weeds, barks, seeds, vegetables, and herbs were employed in treating illnesses, and each had its advocates.

Books labeled "home medical advisors" were numerous, if not always easily accessible in pioneer settlements, but it is quite likely that in considering what books, if any, to take to Oregon or California, anyone who could read might consider one of them. Many of the books contained simplified versions of "regular" medicinal treatments, but there were others that showed pronounced Thomsonian and homeopathic influences. Thomson's *New Guide to Health, or Botanic Family Physician* was popular, but on the other hand, Doctor John C. Gunn's *Domestic Medicine, or Poor Man's Friend, in the House of Affliction, Pain, and Sickness* had sold over 100,000 copies by 1839.

In the forties the regular pioneer doctor possessed a simple *materia medica,* namely, calomel, laudanum, Glauber's salts, Dover's powders, quinine (or Peruvian bark), and jalap. According to the 1830 edition of the *U.S. Pharmacopoeia,* calomel was made by treating mercury metal with "sulphuric acid, muriate of soda, and muriate of ammonia" to produce "submuriate of mercury or protochloride of mercury." Laudanum was defined as tincture of opium, that is, a mixture of opium and ethyl alcohol. Glauber's salts consisted of sodium sulfate. Dover's powders was a mixture of ipecacuanha, opium, and potassium sulfate, and jalap was the powdered tuberous root of a Mexican plant, *Exogonium jalapa.* Calomel was an active purgative, as was Glauber's salts; jalap, laudanum, and opium were used as anodynes. The home medicine cabinet would have included some or all of these plus any of the hundreds of remedies derived from folk sources. One home medical guide advised that the medicine chest should be supplied as follows: 2 oz. calomel, 4 oz. jalap, 4 oz. rhubarb, 2 oz. calcined magnesia, 2 drams powdered gamboge, 4 drams tartar emetic, a bottle of mustard, a pint of tincture of *Lobelia,* 4 drams of quinine, a bottle of castor oil, half-pint sweet spirits of niter, half pint spirits of hartshorn, 2 drams of opium, ½ lb. of nitrite of potash, 2 oz. ipecacuanha, 2 oz. Cayenne pepper, 4 oz. best aloes, 4 oz. Burgundy pitch, a box of blistering plaster, a stick of adhesive plaster, a half pint of laudanum, a pint of spirits of camphor, a cake of Castile soap, 4 oz. senna, 10 lbs. (!) Epsom salts, a pint syringe, a 3-oz. graduated glass, an apothecary's scale and weights, and a small Wedgewood mortar.

The newspapers and almanacs of the forties were well covered with advertisement for all sorts of patent medicines claiming to cure every known ailment of man and beast. Itinerant "doctors," hucksters, local shopkeepers, medicine men, and traveling salesmen were all busily engaged in the business of selling balms, restoratives, elixirs, lotions, pills, salves, bitters, powders, drops, unctions, ointments, essences, lozenges, and specifics. Most of these were worthless, some were harmful, and since there was no regulation of either claims or contents, many found their way into the medicine cabinets and stomachs of the sanguine frontier settlers. They also were carried in the wagons headed over the plains. Many an emigrant probably had stocked away somewhere "Dr. Fahnestock's Celebrated Vermifuge and Liquid Opeldoc"; or "Dr. M. S. Watson's Great Invincible Birgharimi Stiff Joint Panacea"; or "Dr. Felix's Celebrated Liver Pills"; or rattlesnake oil; or worm-destroying lozenges, or a number of other patent medicines. The January, 1840, issues of the *New York Herald* carried advertisements for Hunters Red Drop, Mothe's Capsules, Sterling's Oriental Balsamic Compound, Dr. Jordan's Balsam of Rakasiri, Madam Gardion's Specific for Leucorrhoea, and Dr. Goodman's American Anti-Gonorrhoea Pills—in the venereal category alone!

As late as 1860 only a few wagon trains to the West were lucky enough to have a doctor along. Dr. C.M. Clark, who accompanied a wagon train in the Pike's Peak gold rush, stated: "Every man had a package of drugs and nostrums, with written directions for use, sometimes consisting of blue pills, a little ipecac and opium, together with a bottle of peppermint, pain-killer and somebody's sovereign remedy for all ills." Brandreth's Vegetable Universal Pills were selling at the rate of five thousand boxes daily in 1836. These little gems contained colycinth, aloes, gamboge, soap, peppermint, and cinnamon. Goelicke's Matchless Sanative, while not making universal claims, merely promised to cure consumption, palsy, gout, dropsy, insanity, indigestion, diabetes, jaundice, spine complaint, ague, *delirium tremens,* headache, eye trouble, leprosy, and sickness in pregnancy. It is a wonder, therefore, that anyone armed with these preparations would dare to become ill!

Even if he were in ill health, many an emigrant hoped that the climate of the prairies and the lush and green land of Oregon and California would do wonders in restoring him to vigorous good health; that is, after all, what many had said it would do. Persons going west for health reasons later were described variously as "lungers, consumptives, phthistics, coughers, hackers, invalids, valetudinarians, sanitarians, asthmatics, rheumatics, white plaguers, pukers, and walking death."

5

CAMPING OUT

A revealing and honest description of life on the trail was written by Jesse Applegate in 1843. He described one day's activities of a group of a thousand emigrants headed for Oregon in the "great migration," from 4 A.M., when the sentinels fired their rifles to awaken the sleeping camp, until the 10 P.M. night watch assumed his post. It is a quite ordinary story—no superhuman feats, no Indian raids, just the dusty plodding along of the oxen and wagons mile after mile wearily across the plains. Only one incident broke that day's monotony, namely, when Dr. Marcus Whitman, who was with this group, attended a pregnant woman and delivered her of a healthy child. The doctor's advice as to what to do on the trail was brief: "Travel, travel, travel; nothing else will take you to the end of your journey; nothing is wise that does not help you along; nothing is good for you that causes a moment's delay."

Life on the road generally was dull and monotonous, but not always so. Daily routines of emigrants camping out from early May to the middle of September in the 1840s stand in sharp contrast to those of today's modern camper as he zooms from coast to coast in his T.V.-equipped, air-conditioned, self-contained van, covering distances thirty to forty times faster than any ox-drawn wagon ever did. How did the average emigrant and his family keep themselves clean, take care of their skin, teeth, and hair, go to the toilet, take a bath, prepare meals, wash clothes, protect themselves from heat, cold, rain, and hail? Where did they get their water? What kind of diet did they have?

Fig. 7   *Nooning on the Platte* by Albert Bierstadt. Courtesy of the St. Louis Art Museum.

Fig. 8   *The Emigrant Train Bedding Down for the Night*
by Benjamin Franklin Reinhart. By permission of
the Corcoran Gallery of Art.

These, and many other everyday problems, had to be met under conditions very few modern campers would care to cope with.

A day's travel on the trail was a long day, going on, in good weather, for perhaps seventeen hours. The oxen and other animals had to be rounded up and yoked to the wagons. The latter were arranged in a circle with all the tongues pointing in, and each attached by chains to a wheel of the adjacent wagon, thereby forming a stout barrier to both Indians and livestock. The men corralled the animals and hitched up the wagons, the tents were taken down, blankets stowed; the women prepared breakfast, then cleaned up hurriedly, and by 7 o'clock, in all the wild and clamoring confusion, everyone was supposed to be ready to take his assigned place in the line for the day. About five hours later, or sometimes sooner, the train stopped for "nooning." At this time a midday meal was eaten, drivers checked up on their gear and animals, or relaxed for a few minutes snooze, minor repairs or adjustments were made if necessary, water was taken on if available, and the animals were watered and rested. Towards evening, or if a good location was found in the late afternoon, the train again formed its usual circle of wagons, the oxen were unhitched to graze, hopefully at some grassy site, the horses and mules were tethered, the evening's meal was prepared, and everyone looked forward to a well-deserved rest. Most of the emigrants would be dead tired by this time, but as dusk settled over the train and the campfires blazed away, some irrepressible spirit would start playing a banjo, or a flute, or even a clarinet, or, God forbid, a bugle!

There would be gossip among the women, as well as mending and baking, and those who could, might write letters, hoping to get them sent home somehow, and others would record, sometimes laconically, the day's events in their diaries. "Likes attracted likes," and there were some social lines drawn, even on the plains, the more prosperous emigrants tending to mingle with their own kind, and the poorer with theirs. The men might get into discussions, arguments, or fights, drink, play cards, or attend ailing animals or wagons. A lame animal, or one with hoof troubles, was a serious business. Emigrants became more mindful of the well-being of the animals the farther they traveled, realizing their chances of reaching Oregon and California intact lay in the strong legs and backs of the oxen. Cattle became lame going over prairie grass that had been burned. The sharp stubs irritated the cattle's feet, which would become dry and feverish, with cracks appearing in the hoof opening. These cracks were foci for infections, and had to be washed out with strong soap suds, the diseased flesh was excised with a knife, and boiling pitch or tar poured over the sore area. The reactions of the animals were not recorded but can be imagined.

The young adults might pair off for courting or lovemaking; kids might run and shout, play games, and let off their inexhaustible store of energy—after their chores were done, of course! Everyone would try to clean up a little bit, but often the weary traveler did none of these things; after disposing of his evening meal, he might fall on his India rubber sheet, pull the blanket over his head, and sleep as if dead through the night, unwashed and fully clothed!

In bad weather, such as incessant and driving rainstorms, overpowering heat, or dust storms, even stopping for the night was an uncomfortable and wearying task, superimposed on a myriad of the day's other tiring and difficult ones. Sleeping in wet clothes was no fun; sleeping on the wet ground or in a wet wagon was no fun either, particularly if warm food could not be prepared for the evening meal. After a few weeks of camping out under these conditions, novice travelers might well wonder why they had started in the first place on so dispiriting a journey.

At night all was not necessarily peaceful, either. The whinny of horses, the shuffling of animal feet, or the lowing of cattle, might raise fears that an Indian attack was imminent, though this rarely happened except along the Humboldt River. Then there were the mournful and incessant wolf howls or coyote yappings and barkings to keep a worried emigrant from sleeping soundly. Wolves were particularly disliked because they dug up bodies of the dead, who because of lack of wood had to be buried in shallow graves wrapped only in their blankets. Fresh meat in camp generally attracted wolves, at least when the emigrants were still east of the Rocky Mountains. There were several different kinds of wolves on the prairies, among them the prairie wolf, the gray wolf, and the black wolf. They could be seen skulking around a camp just outside of gunshot range, and they were a constant threat to the animals. It was not wise to take an evening stroll outside the corral at night.

One of the most important items in the daily life of traveling emigrants was water—common, ordinary, drinking water. As long as the trail crossed rivers, streams, and creeks, a supply of some sort, to be carried in water kegs and canteens, generally was assured. On the other hand, in desert regions or areas suffering from drought conditions, water became crucial not only to the emigrants but especially to their animals, particularly those pulling the heavy wagons over sandy stretches in the intense heat. Furthermore, in the hot, dry air of the plains, the wagons began to fall apart; sidings split and wheels warped as the wood shrank.

Sometimes there was too much water, as for example, in the spring months there was usually a rainy belt between the Missouri River and the south fork of the Platte River where wagons were continually getting bogged down in muddy sloughs. Streams became too high to ford, cooking had to be suspended, everything became damp or soaking wet, and in the chill winds that seemed to blow continuously life was indeed miserable. A great rainstorm on the Platte River occurred on May 30, 1849, and accompanied by hurricane winds drove in all directions many cattle that had been put out to graze. Many were lost, and consequently some wagons were left without any animals to pull them, or with too few to make it all the way. Emigrants in this predicament became suddenly and completely dependent for assistance on their fellow emigrants, many of whom were, unfortunately, unable to help them. Bruff[1] wrote:

Rain fell in a perfect sheet, blinding and appalling lightening. In a few seconds from the commencement of this tempest, the hail suddenly descended, like large gravel in immense quantities, thrown down upon us. . . . The Hail-Stones of extraordinary size, not only cut and bruised the men, whose faces and hands were bleeding, but it also cut the mules. I thought that in my younger days, in the tropics, and at sea, I had seen some tall storms, but this one beat all in my experience.

It was not always possible to find a nearby stream to camp next to as darkness approached, so one had to get water where and when one could. Water-filled buffalo-wallow holes, hollows, puddles, and sloughs were used as sources. Around many campsites in the Platte River valley, shallow wells were dug, and often these would fill up with cool clean water of a much better quality than that from the muddy Platte itself. As the wagon trains moved farther west, water became less abundant and of poorer quality. Tadpoles and minnows might have to be screened

---

[1]   G. W. Read and R. Gaines (eds.), *Gold Rush: The Journals, Drawings, and Other Papers of J[oseph] Goldsborough Bruff,* pp. 47–48 (July 20, 1849).

out of Platte River water, and other sources might be muddy, but alkaline salts such as sodium borate, sodium sulfate, sodium, magnesium, and potassium carbonates, as well as dissolved hydrogen sulfide, could not be sieved out, and many a thirsty emigrant drank terrible-tasting water or did not drink at all. Coffee, and all other foods prepared from such chemically-tainted water, acquired peculiar flavors and odors of their own, and often it required fierce appetites to swallow these foods and keep them down. Water containing high concentrations of alkaline salts had a severe purgative effect on the intestinal tract, and some emigrants suffered continuously from the debilitating effects of these natural laxatives. Sometimes it was humanly impossible to prevent thirsty animals from rushing to drink the nearest water and dying as a consequence of its poisonous effects. One remedy for "alkalied" animals was to give them a "nicotine sandwich," that is, a plug of tobacco placed between two slices of bacon forced down their throats with a blunt stick. Vinegar also was used for treating poisoned animals. After the animals drank alkali water, saliva would flow freely from their mouths; they began to swell, grow weak and tremble, and soon would fall to the ground and die.

Some water sources along the trail acquired a notoriety and were constantly mentioned, particularly Soda Springs and Beer Springs on the Fort Hall Road. The waters of these springs were saturated with carbon dioxide gas and were considered to be as refreshing as soda water. Some emigrants added lemon syrup to them, thereby making lemon soda, a rare drink for a place as isolated as the springs were.

On the journey to California emigrants usually traveled down the sullen and desolate Humboldt River, following it through the Nevada desert country to its sink. Pritchard[2] described it as

. . . a vast plain over which the water spreads gradually or loses itself in the sand. It is a vast Quagmire or Marsh of Stagnant Saline and Alkali water mixed, and emits a most offensive and nauseating effluvia . . . . There is nothing of the appearance of a Lake about it, as you can only see the water in spots. It therefore has the appearance of Ponds[rather] than of a Lake. Takeing it all in all, it is one of the most disagreeable and loathsome looking places on the face of the earth.

---

[2]   D.L. Morgan (ed.), *The Overland Diary of James A. Pritchard from Kentucky to California in 1849*, p. 122.

Sometimes desperate with thirst, emigrants would throw blankets into the "best looking" water, then squeeze them out into a container in the hope of procuring something drinkable; however, many would only retch and vomit up this black, thick, nauseous fluid.

The waters of rivers and swift-flowing streams were serious obstacles for the emigrants. Ordinarily, if a stream was not too deep, a few feet or so, and if the bottom were pebbly or rocky, wagons could simply ford across them, as at Independence Crossing on the Big Blue, and California Crossing on the Platte. In other cases, where the bottoms were full of potholes, or quicksand, or the stream ran deep and swift, other measures were needed. The livestock usually were forced to swim over slow-running rivers or streams, but the Laramie, the Green, the Snake, and other strong rivers, were formidable challenges to both man and beast, and both often lost. There were few usable bridges, but several ferries were established by enterprising pioneers; the one at the North Platte entrance to the Sweetwater valley, built and operated by the Mormons, was well known to emigrants. There was a fee, of course, for both wagons and animals. In order to get families and goods over rivers, and to lighten the load on wagons that had to be floated, bullboats were used for transporting them. Directions for constructing a bullboat were given by John Ball:[3]

A "bullboat" is made of willow branches twelve to fourteen feet long, each about one and a half inches at the butt end. These ends were fixed in the ground in converging rows at proper distances from each other, and as they approached nearer the ends the branches were brought nearer together so as to form something of a bow. The ends of the whole were brought together like ribs of a great basket; and then they took other twigs of willow and wove them into those stuck in the ground so as to make a sort of firm, long, huge basket. After this was completed they sewed together a number of buffalo skins and with them covered the whole; and after the different parts had been trimmed off smooth, a slow fire was made under the "bullboat" taking care to dry the skins moderately; and as they gradually dried and acquired a due degree of heat they rubbed buffalo tallow all over the outside of it so as to allow it to enter into the seams of the concern, now no longer a willow basket. As the melted tallow ran down into every seam, hold and crevice, it cooled into a firm body, capable of resisting the water and bearing a considerable blow without damage.

---

[3] J. Ball, "Across the Continent Seventy Years Ago," Extracts from the journal of John Ball in his trip across the Rocky Mountains and his life in Oregon, N. N. B. Powers (ed.), *Oregon Historical Quarterly* 2 (1902): 82–106.

Wagons could be floated if their beds were waterproofed, and some logs were lashed along the bottom or sides, but this maneuver was dangerous and new for most emigrants. Sometimes wagons were floated over rivers on top of crude rafts of logs which had been lashed together, and poled across, or else guided over by ropes stretched across the river. Long lines of waiting wagons usually were headed for ferry sites, and often a train would wait all day, or even several days, before being able to use a particularly crowded one. Drownings were frequent among men trying to swim their stock across in the face of strong currents, and stories of wagons getting stuck and lost in quicksand, or turning over, or being carried away and smashed downstream are not uncommon in accounts of pioneer attempts at crossing rivers.

On June 13, 1844, an emigrant[4] wrote in his diary about crossing the Big Blue.

The plan of swimming the cattle was for the guides—four or five—to go in ahead, each with a strong ox, and take the lower side of the animal, holding to him with the hand by the withers, and cuff his cheek if necessary to guide him to the going out place. But this proved hazardous. Without thinking of the suck-holes, I went to the lead ox, but before I had time to get to his head, he was taken right down by one of the whirlpools. Thinking I could save myself and not hinder the beast, I took my hand from him. Then the water clutched and pulled me under. By a desperate effort, I kept my eyes out, so that I could see the boys and men on the bank. But far quicker than it can be told, I was carried down to another swirl, and again taken down, without being able to take a breath, and as I went I saw a boy start for camp. I was struggling with all my might, and fully realized my danger. No, I did not pass in review my sins, as I have read of; I did seem to see my mother weeping for me. Yet there was another thought in me, I would go down and dive for the main current. As this passed like a flash, I felt something touch my right side, and put out my hand—finding the object to be the back of an ox, which by superior strength had overtaken and was passing me. This enabled me to get to the surface and breathe. How restful it was just to keep my hold. He was aiming at the proper point, and after resting a little, I swam back, below the eddy, thinking I would trust the courage and strength of an ox in the future. I was twice reported drowned that day.

---

[4]   J. Minto, "Reminiscences of Honorable John Minto, Pioneer of 1844," *Oregon Historical Quarterly* 2 (1901): 121–67, 210–54. Minto incorporated a journal written by the Reverend E.E. Parrish into his account, and it is the latter's words that are quoted here.

Taking a bath presented problems to the Victorian-minded emigrants. They were likely to be dirty and odoriferous after many hard
days of driving in dust and heat without bathing. Best to approach
them from the windward side—especially the men, the "bull-whackers,"
guides, and others who did the hard and sweaty physical jobs! They
and their clothes would likely be covered with alkali, dust, mud, dung,
grime, and muck from their daily walk and—sooner or later—they
would have to get their clothes laundered and bodies cleaned. Most of
the time washing consisted of a brief splash of water over the face,
head, and hands. Getting a bath was something else, perhaps attended
to at intervals of weeks, and this luxury was afforded only when camping was done near a stream or river.

The word "bath" meant different things to different people, and
some baths were taken without the preliminary of removing all the un-
derclothing! Then there was the question of modesty to consider, and
preferably the males had to take their baths at one place and the females at another—and maybe not at the same time. The water of
streams and rivers was generally cold, sometimes icily cold, and this did
not encourage lingering in it, or help make stiff joints and sore muscles
feel any better. Commercial soaps were available in the forties, but the
harsh, farm-made, boiled alkali ash-and-tallow balls or bars of "soap"
were used most frequently. In the forties commercially prepared soap
was manufactured from coconut, palm, babassu, sesame, olive, or soy-
bean oil. Homemade soap was made from household fats, which were
boiled together with lye made from wood ashes. It was a yellow colored product and strongly alkaline. Together with a rough cloth or bris-
tle brush, and the bracing cold water, a bath could be an invigorating
tonic to a bone-weary traveler in hot weather. However, frequent baths
and the fetish for cleanliness that modern American society has es-
poused were not yet in evidence, and even in the cities, "once a week" in
the summer was considered adequate. There were, of course, no anti-
perspirants, and deodorants were merely a few cosmetic perfumes and
powders. Hair also was washed with the same coarse soap, although
some commercially prepared shampoos were available. It must have
been extremely difficult to obtain a good lather in hard-water regions,
although some emigrants reported that in places stream water was soft-
er than rain water. It was equally difficult to remove the precipitated
alkali soap clots from long hair and beards; they had to be combed out.
All things considered, washing one's hair outdoors was an onerous and

messy, if not hopeless, task. Although in the 1830s the average man was clean shaven, most of the emigrant males soon were adorned with beards and long hair because of the exigencies of trail life. The effects of harsh alkali soap on cracked, blistered, raw hands and feet, and on sun- and windburned arms, faces, and necks must have been brutal.

Water was necessary for anyone wishing to clean his mouth or brush his teeth. On the trail teeth might occasionally be cleaned by rubbing with a rough linen cloth or a piece of mallow root, or picked with a pointed stick or other toothpick. Soot and other abrasives were popular tooth cleaners, and recipes for homemade dentifrices advised tobacco ashes mixed with honey; charcoal; areca nuts; orris root; and cuttlefish bone. There were brushes for teeth, but they were of uncertain sanitary condition, and not used regularly. In the forties, the state of American teeth was bad, and dentistry was appallingly primitive. All dental work was done by hand, perhaps as a sideline by a regular doctor, perhaps by anyone who liked to do that sort of thing on a part-time basis. Rotten teeth were hand-drilled, as much as the patient could stand, and then filled with materials such as wood, tin, lead, or gold. These fillings would soon fall out or rot (in the case of wood) and the patient was as badly off as before. Essence of peppermint or other "scents" were used to mask the formidable odors arising from mouths of unbrushed and rotted teeth. If a tooth had to be pulled, any handy pliers or similar tool was used to yank it out; if the tooth had rotted to the gumline, and perhaps was abscessed, the patient probably suffered unbearable pain from which there was little lasting relief. Four or five months on the trail with tooth trouble all the way would have required a strong-willed personality to endure it, even with the help of opium, whiskey, and cotton plugs dipped in essential oils of cloves or mustard, or pyroligneous acid stuffed in the cavities. The bark from the "toothache tree" (southern prickly ash) produces a curious cooling sensation when chewed, and it also was used as an anaesthetic for toothache pain.

Going to the toilet while the train was moving along was a difficult operation. Many emigrants hinted that they experienced almost constant diarrhoea or dysentery while on the trail. A combination of poor food poorly prepared and the laxative salts in drinking water probably accounted for most of these cases. In any event, a man or woman or child suffering from this malady could hardly be expected to wait until "nooning," or until the night's campsite had been set before relieving his griping bowels or bladder. Some wagons were equipped with slop buckets where in the press of circumstances one could relieve oneself. This arrangement was probably necessary on the broad and treeless plains, where not even a sagebush was around to provide sufficient privacy for the exercises of necessary bodily functions. Of course, there was no soap or water out there with which to wash up afterwards, so that any fecal or urinary contamination of hands and clothes remained for some time. The terrible spread of trail epidemics of cholera, typhoid, and dysentery was likely aided by the transmission of bacteria through very poor personal toilet habits. Toilet paper was first manufactured in 1857, and it may be left to the reader's conjecture as to how sanitary operations following evacuation of loose bowels were carried out. Toilet paper made from unbleached, pearl-colored, pure manila hemp paper was first manufactured in New York City by Joseph C. Gayetty. His name was watermarked on each sheet, and a packet consisted of five hundred sheets for fifty cents. It was marketed as "Gayetty's Medicated Paper—a pure article for the toilet and for prevention of piles." Dried broad leaves? Old papers? Nothing? In any case, a five months supply could not be brought along, and the trail itself offered very little for the emigrants' bodily comfort. Mormon leaders insisted that defecation take place a good distance away from their campsites, and that all feces had to be buried. There is very little evidence available as to the toilet habits of emigrants when camping overnight. The nearest sagebush or a canvas screen probably served for a urinal, and beyond that we can only speculate on what they did with the slop buckets.

Clothes were laundered whenever a train happened to stop for the night by a convenient water source and time was available for the job. Obviously, the dirty clothes could accumulate for some time between washings. Mountain men had their own system of cleaning their clothes and blankets. After they were well infested with lice or "graybacks," garments were removed to a thriving anthill, where they were spread out and allowed to remain all day. The ants conveniently took care of all the lice for their own purposes, and after a few shakes the clothes were ready to wear again; deloused but not necessarily de-scented. Having lice was a common complaint on the plains and attests to the infrequency of bathing. Indian women scattered pungent prairie wormwood and silver sage among their bed robes, and deloused them

by hanging over racks exposed to a thick smudge from burning sage-
wood and sweet grass. There is no mention, to my knowledge, of how
emigrant women "sweetened" their bedding. Dirty garments usually
were thrown into a pond or stream, soaped, rubbed and kneaded, then
rinsed and hung out in the sun to dry. It was a difficult job what with
cold water, obdurate stains and dirt, and bad soap; also very hard on
the knuckles! Laundry was hardly ever tub-boiled, because of lack of
tubs and the trouble and time required to carry out this operation.
When the weather was wet, laundering was impossible, and even if it
were possible, the clothes would not dry; when the weather was dry,
there might not be water available, or else the dust deposited on the
garments hung to dry dirtied them all over again. There was, of course,
no ironing done, but even so, a woman's lot seemed to be one onerous
chore after another, day after day. Narcissa Whitman arrived at Fort
Boise six months after leaving her home in New York in order to go to
Oregon with her husband, Dr. Marcus Whitman. In her diary she wrote,
"Last night I put my clothes in water, and this morning finished washing before breakfast; this is the third time I have washed since I left
home, once at Ft. William (on the Laramie) and once at Rendezvous
(on the Green R.)."

The diet and cooking practices on the trail have been described
by many emigrants, and it is no wonder that many remarked about having dyspepsia, "colik," or uneasy stomachs as they jostled along. On
the trail cooking food was a problem from the start, and the novelty
of "eating out" soon wore off as the monotony of the diet began im-
pressing itself on the emigrants' stomachs. Among the items listed as
foods eaten by the pioneers one finds: acorn porridge, antelope, atole,
bacon, beans, bear, bear grease pies, beaver, beef, boudine, bread, buffalo, buttermilk, cactus, chicken, chili peppers, chocolate, cider, coffee,
corn, crackers, currants, deer, dog meat, dry vegetables, eggs, elk, fish,
flour, fowl, fruits, game, goats, grass seeds, ham, hawk, honey, horse
meat, hunter's pudding, insects, jerked meat, liver, lizards, macaroni,
mesquite beans, milk, molasses, mule meat, mutton, ox meat, penole,
pine nuts, pork, porridge, prairie chicken, prairie dog, pumpkin, rabbit,
raccoon, rattlesnake, rawhide, rice, roots, rose buds, sage hen, salt, sau-
sage, skunk, soup, sugar, tea, toads, tortillas, tule roots, turkey, turtle,
vegetables, wolf, and worms.[5] The hearty appetites engendered by the

---

[5]   L.R. and A.W. Hafen (eds.), *The Far West and Rockies Series,* vol. 15 (Glendale, Calif.: Clark, 1961).

fresh air and hard work on the trail were somewhat blunted when after
the first few weeks the food brought from back east had given out, and
the trail menu commenced and was continued indefinitely thereafter.

Heating food required using dry buffalo chips or dried prairie
grass, since wood was very scarce on the plains, but it was possible to
build a sort of fireplace and thereby have a hot meal. One method was
described as follows:

[At] a spot a short distance from the steep river bank, a hole about six
inches in diameter and eight to twelve inches deep was excavated. An
air tunnel was then formed by forcing a ramrod horizontally from the
river bank to the bottom of the cavity, giving the oven the required
draught. In making a fire (after gathering a quantity of dry chips,
which were found in abundance), a wisp of dry grass was lighted and
placed at the bottom of the oven, opposite the air tunnel, feeding the
flame with finely pulverized dry chips, which readily ignited. Then after filling the fireplace with broken chips and placing around the oven
two or three small rocks on which to rest the cooking utensils, we had
a combination which at first gave us a grand surprise, as but little
smoke and only slight odor emitted from the fire, and we found, after
having eaten our first meal cooked in this manner, that the prejudice
entertained against buffalo chips as fuel had vanished into thin air."

Some emigrants said that buffalo chip smoke imparted a "pep-
pery flavor" to their food. A fireplace of the sort described above was
not, however, feasible on flat plains, or in rocky or desert conditions,
and here the utensils had to be suspended above the fire in some manner, either from a tripod, or by placing them on a legged platform. It
should also be noted that as the altitude increased, water boiled at a
lower temperature—and cooking results were not the same as those at
lower altitudes.

American eating habits were often gross, and the rule of "gulp,
gobble, and go" was often adhered to at meal times. In his book *The
American Democrat* James Fenimore Cooper wrote:

The Americans are the grossest feeders of any civilized nation known.
As a nation, their food is heavy, coarse, ill-prepared and indigestible,
while it is taken in the least artificial form that cooking will allow. The
predominance of grease in the American kitchen, coupled with habits
of hasty eating and of constant expectoration, are the causes of the diseases of the stomach so common in America.

An ordinary breakfast back home in the forties might consist of boiled eggs, a meat dish such as bacon, sausages, or beef, oatmeal or cornmeal mush, toast or hot bread of some sort, butter, potatoes, and coffee or tea. On the trail the two staples were "sowbelly and biscuit," and these were supplemented with a liquid of varying composition and taste called "coffee." The bread was tough and the coffee was corrosive, and in between, any and all other kinds of food were consumed in no particular order at any given meal. Fried bacon, boiled beans, molasses, crackers, chokeberries, gooseberries, currants, and wild onions, buffalo, antelope, game birds, fish, parched corn and dried vegetables, sometimes made into soup, and perhaps milk and butter, if the emigrant had brought a cow or two along, was the usual menu to be expected for four or five months. The "bass" of the buffalo, a projection just before the shoulders, was removed with the skin attached; it was generally prepared by boiling, and was said to resemble marrow, being both nutritious and delicious to taste. The hump, hump ribs, and tongue were also considered among the best portions of the animal. When buffalo were plentiful, often this was all that was removed, and the remainder of the carcass was left for the wolves. It must be added that it was not too long before game animals, and even birds and fish, as well as the berries, were only infrequently met with, the former having learned to avoid the trail, and the latter having been completely consumed by continuous and voracious streams of hungry emigrants. If game was desired, it had to be gotten by a hunting party foraging at some distance from the main party. This could be dangerous.

Diets were overloaded with carbohydrates and fats, and with some exceptions, too low on proteins. Citrus fruits and vegetables, as well as eggs and milk products, were not much in evidence, and apparently the emigrants carried what they hoped would keep them going the longest. There were, of course, cases of scurvy, and other forms of malnutrition on the trail—probably babies and children suffered most from various critical dietary deficiencies, especially those affecting teeth formation and bone development. At the end of the meal dishes would be washed with water, but iron pots and skillets were scoured out with wood ashes or sand.

There was some drinking, and in a few cases a lot, such as on the Fourth of July, but generally the emigrants took along a little whiskey or brandy for medicinal purposes. The word "whiskey" meant almost anything; watered mixtures of diluted raw alcohol and tobacco and pepper were sold to the Indians, but also drunk by mountain men. One recipe for the "Montana blend" of whiskey was as follows: "One qt. raw alcohol, 1 lb. rank black chewing tobacco, 1 bottle Jamaica ginger, 1 handful red pepper, 1 qt. black molasses, Missouri River water as required." The pepper and tobacco were boiled together, and when these were nearly cool the other ingredients were added; the mixture was then stirred with a willow stick, and the alcohol added last. The "skull varnish" of Missouri—a mixture of molasses and opalescent "undistilled whiskey" was unique. In the West of the forties the per capita consumption of whiskey was estimated to have been about 5 gallons per year,

One of the most irritating things the traveling emigrants had to endure was the dust. The soil was parched by the sun and reduced to a powder by the long trains of wagons, while the sagebushes prevented the making of new tracks. A strong wind blew from the West, and there was no escaping the dust. The emigrants had to eat, drink, and breathe it. The dust on the trail was so fine that the slightest disturbance raised it up, and the wagon trains produced clouds so dense that sometimes visibility was reduced to less than 10 feet. The alkali dust was said to blister and blotch the lips so that the travelers all appeared to have been touched with poison ivy. It also had a powerful effect on the eyes, throat, and lungs, filling the former with burning tears, and making breathing difficult, saturating the mouth with granular material having a bitter acrid taste, and drying out the membranous passages of the nose. The scalp became powdery and the hair dry as straw, every line and crevice of the body was etched out as it was filled in with dust, almost impervious to scrubbing out, the clothes all took on a suffocating smell, and sweat droplets and tears turned to muddy rivulets as they coursed down the face and body. The animals suffered as much as the people, and when intolerable heat was superimposed on the dust, a picture of suffering worthy of Dante's imagination emerges. The heat tended to bake burning crusts of dust on the animals' ears, eyelids, and nostrils, and it is a wonder they kept from going mad. Some did go mad. The emigrants tied handkerchiefs over their mouths and noses, and placed curtains across the front opening of their wagons in vain efforts to avoid suffocating effects of dust. Wagon trains daily rotated the position of each wagon so that eventually, and for at least a day, a wagon would lead, and hence, be ahead of most of the dust. Pity the emigrants in the last wagon under these conditions! Everything not tightly sealed and protected was slowly infiltrated with dust, and gritty food was to be expected after going over dusty roads for a few days. Many emigrants said that the people back east would never know what a dusty road was really like until they traveled over one along the trail to the West. Truly they looked like an army of dun-colored ghosts.

When the sun was shining brightly on a cloudless day, the emigrants suffered from glare and eyestrain. Going over a salt desert produced the same effects on the eyes as going over a snowfield, and Frémont remarked that glare, combined with great fatigue, had rendered many persons nearly blind. In the Sierra Nevadas some of Frémont's men wore black silk handkerchiefs as veils, and this procedure very much relieved their eyes. Sore and bloodshot eyes were washed with weak solutions, if available, of silver nitrate or zinc sulfate, or with warm milk, or even plain warm water. Some medical guides recommended that poultices made of light bread and milk, as cold as possible, be applied to the eyes. Broad-brimmed hats and poke-bonnets were worn to give some measure of protection from the glare and bright sun, but these were also hot, and soon became saturated with sweat. In the fifties some travelers to the West began to wear goggles as a protection from the dust.

Mirages are common in arid lands, and many emigrants had not experienced them before coming west. They are especially cruel because on deserts they give the illusion of bodies of water. Edwin Bryant[6] described what he saw in the deserts of Utah and Nevada:

The mirage, a beautiful phenomenon, I have frequently mentioned as exhibiting itself upon our journey, here displayed its wonderful illusions, in a perfection and with a kind of magnificence surpassing any presentation of the kind I have previously seen. Lakes, dotted with islands and bordered by groves of gently waving timber, whose tranquil and limpid waves reflected their sloping banks and the shady islets in their bosoms, lay spread out before us, inviting us, by their illusionary temptations, to stray from our path and enjoy their cooling shades and refreshing waters.

[6] E. Bryant, *What I Saw in California: Being the Journal of a Tour by the Emigrant Route and South Pass of the Rocky Mountains of North America, the Great Desert Basin, and through California in the Years 1846 and 1847* (London: Routledge, 1849).

Sunset was often a welcomed sight.

Another of the irritants often encountered was insects—buffalo gnats, mosquitoes, and June bugs being most frequently mentioned; ordinary flies are not often cited. Around the Green River one pioneer wrote that "mosquitoes settled on the mules like a swarm of bees on a sour apple tree, and the poor animals were frantic." The emigrants secured the beasts to wagon wheels and then built fires of chaparral in order to smoke the insects out, but when this did not work, they melted bacon grease into which they dipped the most offensive smelling herbs they could find and applied this to the mules from head to tails. Some relief was afforded by this procedure.

Elisha Perkins wrote in his diary for July 9, 1849, that

the Buffaloe gnats are so annoying that I can hardly write getting into my eyes nose mouth & ears in swarms & when they light biting almost as bad as mosquitoes. One of our mules was brot up a few mornings since so badly bitten by them as to be swelled in places large as my two fists.

Bryant also remarked about the ferocity of mosquitoes; often, in order to avoid them, the emigrants would yoke up before daylight and hope to be rid of them. Horseflies also were observed to bite ferociously and without discrimination. Another pioneer said that on the Bannock River beyond Fort Hall "our Fourth of July was spent in traveling in the dust and in fighting off musketoes. Their attacks were more fearce and determined, and more numerous, along this river, than any of the kind I ever witnessed." The emigrants had nothing in the way of insect repellents, and their faces and hands were often covered with great welts as they passed through a mosquito belt. Some emigrants mentioned the presence of scorpions and tarantula spiders in their encampments but by this time, usually along the Humboldt River, their capacity for reaction had been ground down considerably.

Constant exposure to intense sun and dry wind caused painful cracking of the lips, nose, and fingers. These sore and nagging hurts never seemed to heal. The irritation to the hands was compounded by continuous exposure to alkali dust that burned into them, and by the rough work in handling oxen and doing other hard chores. A number of ointments were in existence for treating these conditions, including as well cases of sun- and windburn. Basilicum ointment was made from 1 oz. beeswax, 1 oz. resin, and 1½ oz. clean lard. For burns, 3 grains of morphine acetate could be mixed in with 1 oz. basilicum ointment, and applied to the affected area with the feather end of a quill. For chapped hands, boiled potatoes were thought to be efficacious, and also to keep the skin soft and healthy. Other medical guides had a number of remedies, including smearing the afflicted skin with warm mutton tallow, or fresh oil of sweet almonds, then covering with a soft rag. When the inflammation left, the skin was bathed in brandy, "diluted to such a degree with water as not to smart." Another recipe called for 1 oz. pure olive oil, half a dram of yellow beeswax; these two mixed together by melting the latter with gentle heat, then stirring in 1 dram new honey, and half a dram of white flowers of zinc. When cold, this lotion was briskly rubbed into the skin and the part then wiped with a soft towel. Olive oil, sweet oil, and poultices of raw Irish potatoes, carrots, or turnips, were also recommended by various authorities for burns and scalds.

Sore joints and muscles were a frequent complaint of emigrants, and for this Doctor Frisbee's suggested treatment is interesting. One procured one gill each of angleworms, neatsfoot oil, and brandy, and "simmered them together moderately." The mixture then was ready for use, and it was applied morning and night by the fire; thereafter the treated part was kept wrapped up. Sore feet were a common complaint on the trail, particularly when the road was over rocky and hard terrain and shoes, if any, were wearing thin. Boots chafed and blistered the feet, and moccasins were little protection from rock bruises and punctures, or from burning hot sands. It must be remembered that most of the emigrants walked nearly all of the time. One of the liniments hopefully carried along had to suffice in really bad cases, but most of the time the feet were just soaked in a nearby stream of cold water, if possible; if not, a bucket or tub of water had to do, and when water was scarce, there was nothing. A rheumatic liniment was recommended for sprains, bruises, rheumatic pains, swellings, etc.

Take the best hand soap—1 oz, camphor—1 oz, very strong spirit—1 pt; mix the soap with the spirit and let stand in moderate heat until the soap is dissolved, occasionally shaking the phial, then add the camphor and 1 teaspoonful of cayenne [pepper], and also 1 teaspoonful of turpentine; shake until dissolved.

Sticks of adhesive plasters were available, and these could have been used for protecting foot blisters from being rubbed raw.

Some emigrants had frightening experiences with rattlesnakes on the trail, although few actually were bitten. Alonzo Delano wrote of his experience:

> ... as I jumped over a little gully, my ears were saluated [sic] with a terrible hissing noise. Looking forward about six feet, I saw a monstrous hissing snake, with its head elevated from the ground at least two feet, its eyes flashing with anger, and apparently in the act of springing upon me. ... I jumped aside about six feet, and then, ashamed of my own cowardice, I sprang towards him, as he was elevating his head still higher ... and brought him a blow with my trusty cane which set the monster to groveling in the dust. ... He was over six feet long.

On the other hand, some emigrants felt a wholesome dread of rattlesnakes and felt that they were always on the offensive and hunting for prey, and could spring great lengths and fasten their fangs in their flesh, causing death almost immediately; but most rattlers were only about thirty inches long, and tended to avoid the emigrants as much as possible.

There were, of course, many interesting and exciting new things for the travelers to see. Nearly every diarist and letter writer remarked on the spectacular scenery along the Rocky Mountains, and the beauty and peace of sunsets on the plains. Most of them mentioned Court House Rock, Jail Rock, Chimney Rock, Scott's Bluff, Independence Rock, Devil's Gap, Soda Springs, and other sights along the way. The apparently inexhaustible herds of bison, the colorful, if dirty and sometimes thieving, Indians, the waterfalls, the deserts, the canyons and the swift rivers, new flowers and birds, all supplied the travelers with visual delights and experiences.

Joseph E. Ware in his *Emigrant's Guide to California* (1849) advised the pioneers to "never travel on the Sabbath; we will guarantee that if you lay by on the Sabbath, and rest yourselves and teams, that you will get to California 20 days sooner than those who travel seven days in the week." For churchgoing Christians this advice was heeded for a while, and there might be hymn singing, Bible reading, and a day of comparative rest; but as supplies became short, and competition for available grass and water became fiercer, most emigrants traveled every day, Sunday included. Emigrants did celebrate the Fourth of July with appropriate toasts and salutes from guns and rifles. The pioneers did stop to repair their wagons, pick up supplies and medicines, regroup, and get information about the trail conditions when they came to one of the "forts" along the way. Forts Kearny, Laramie, Bridger, Hall, and Boise were stopping places, and except for the first were originally trading posts. All were primitive and hardly merited the term "fort." It was at Fort Laramie that repacking became a grim necessity if the rougher country ahead was to be crossed, and there was a general abandonment of supplies. Hulbert[7] observed:

The Blackhills [an early name for the Laramie Mountains] so-called because the pine trees give them a somber look against the parched face of the desert, form a rough country, threaded by the southern tributaries of the North Platte, the Bonte, Wagonhound, Prele, Deer, and other creeks; across them our California Road winds and twists in a course that discourages men and beasts to the nth degree. This becomes increasingly evident from the amount of baggage and camp equipment we find cast out on the roadside. In fact, we saw today for the first time vehicles broken up and burned. We once passed the half-consumed fragments of about a dozen wagons, and near them was piled up, in one heap, from six to eight hundredweight of bacon, thrown away for want of horsepower to transport it further. Boxes, bonnets, trunks, wagon wheels, whole wagon bodies, cooking utensils, and in fact almost every article of household furniture were found discarded for the same reason.

Emigrants talked of "seeing the Elephant." This animal was still formidable and unusual, if believable, and attracted attention wherever exhibited. The elephant was the symbol of something different, of something awesome, a great adventure into the unknown. No one really knew what the future held for them on the trail, there was a certain feeling, sometimes bordering on fear or terror, that daily experiences seemed to reinforce, perhaps much like the feeling one might expect if he came face to face for the first time with an elephant in tropical Africa.

---

7   Hulbert, *The Forty-Niners*, p. 121.

6

IN THE VALLEY OF THE SHADOW

The emigrants of the forties often were beset with physical problems. Most likely they had bad teeth, a bad diet, and bad bowels, and were marked externally, internally, or both, by having suffered from a series of periodic diseases that had drained them of stamina and strength. If a man was still young at twenty-five he was old at forty, and the physical experiences on the trail accelerated the aging process. Furthermore, there were hazards, compounded by the exigencies of overland travel, that sooner or later one might not be able to avoid. The difficulties and inconveniences of camping out were one thing, but diseases on the trail such as cholera, dysentery, typhoid, and smallpox, or something like a gunshot wound, a broken arm or leg, and other traumatic and lacerating wounds, or scurvy, or insanity, were something different—they were to be feared because there was little chance for help.

On the trail there were no anaesthetics, no instruments for surgery except ordinary knives and saws, few medicines, and hardly anyone with enough medical knowledge to use them intelligently. The only hope one had was to keep healthy and avoid accidents; it wasn't easy. Estimates suggest that from 1842 to 1859 there were about 20,000 who died on the entire two thousand miles of the Overland Trail, or an average of 10 graves to each mile. If one assumed a total emigration of 350,000, this would average one death for every 17 persons who started.

Back east, the chief endemic communicable diseases were enteritis in the summer months and respiratory infections in the winter. The

Midwest and South still had "ague" or malaria, but pulmonary tuberculosis was "captain of the men of death." Smallpox continued as an important disease in the United States as late as the 1860s. Rheumatism also was a common complaint, and this was to be expected amongst the pioneer settlers who not only suffered much from exposure to the elements, but who were probably ailing from chronic localized infections such as abscessed teeth and bad tonsils.

Before 1849 a relatively small number of people were involved in the trans-Mississippi emigration, and hence epidemics involving great numbers were not possible; perhaps, too, emigrants were healthier. More people had accidents on the trail than diseases in the years prior to 1849. At the advent of the California gold rush, with thousands of adventurers, prospectors, and miners all rushing west, the stage was set for an epidemic on a grand scale. Cholera initially struck the United States in 1832–34, again in 1848–49, and thereafter each year between 1849 and 1854, and finally twice more in 1866 and 1873. Cholera is an intestinal disease caused by a bacterium, *Vibrio cholerae,* and it is spread in the dejecta of an infected human alimentary tract by contaminating food and water, which is then consumed by other susceptible persons. The causative agent was discovered by Robert Koch in 1883; no one in the forties realized anything about the relationship of bacteria to disease.

An attack of cholera might begin in one of two ways. It could supervene in what was considered to be an ordinary case of diarrhoea, or it could appear suddenly without any warning. One doctor of the time described the dramatic symptoms of this dreadful disease:

. . . the changed voice, the *vox cholerica,* consisting in nothing but a mere whisper without all tone and strength, the hollow sunken eye with a black halo, the sharp-pointed ice-cold nose, the continual audible rolling of the gas in the bowels, the cramps in the legs, the asphyate condition, the paralytic condition of the skin, which will keep standing if elevated, above all, the unquenchable thirst, with a cold-pointed tongue, a continual effort to vomit or purge, of what? of a rice-water stool, colorless, odorless.

No wonder the emigrants called this disease the King of Destruction, or the Terror of the Plains! In untreated cholera cases the fatality rate may exceed 50 percent.

It is difficult to imagine what the pioneers did for and to cholera victims in a prairie schooner setting. Their diaries are brief and barren of details. If the weather was nice, the victim might be laid out upon the ground, hopefully in some shady spot. If the weather was bad, and the victim had to be kept in the wagon, cleaning up the vomitus and rice-water stools, whose issue the patient could not control, must have been a nightmare. One can only speculate on what it was like if the victim was kept in a moving wagon. Furthermore, the family and friends in attendance almost certainly exposed themselves to infected materials, and indeed this is one way in which it can be spread. Nothing much is said specifically about the bed-sufferings and agonies of cholera victims in pioneer accounts.

As to causes, doctors of the time were at variance in their beliefs, as usual. The signal work of John Snow in London on cholera was first published in 1849, and his epidemiological studies clearly implicated *something* in the intestinal tract of cholera victims that was being transferred to the healthy, but this was not appreciated for a long time. In general, medical men blamed bad air, noxious exhalations, atmospheric conditions, "animalculae," and bad eating and drinking habits, among other things, as inciting cholera. To avoid cholera, one Dr. Rigdon advised:

Try to keep in good health and take prompt care of bowel and stomach disorders by putting the feet in hot ashes and water, taking ten grains of calomel and one of opium, covering up in bed with hot bricks and boiled ears of corn, and using warm mint tea inside and mustard poultices outside the stomach.

To the pious, however, it was chastisement for national sin.

The 1849 cholera epidemic traveled up the Mississippi River from New Orleans, and thence via the Missouri River to Independence and St. Joseph. Cholera broke out among passengers on the river boats, and indeed emergency stops along the route had to be made to bury the dead. It is obvious that emigrants were certain to harbor the infection with them as they headed west. Cholera is a warm-weather disease, but it is transmitted by neither animals, biting insects, nor the air. Although dissemination from person to person directly is a relatively unimportant route of transmission now, it may not have been in the forties. After 1849 every source of water on the trail could be suspected of being contaminated with cholera organisms. The incubation period varies from a few hours to as long as five days, two to three days being the usual time.

Thus, a person might eat food infected with cholera organisms the evening before leaving Independence, and then some forty or sixty miles out on the trail develop symptoms of the disease.

Grave counts from the border towns to Fort Laramie indicated that fewer than 200 died, or perhaps less than 2 percent of total emigrants going overland in 1849. On the other side, some historians think that more than five thousand emigrants may have been its victims. Regardless of the exact number, which never will be known, cholera was one of the chief deadly fears in the minds of gold seekers and all emigrants in 1849 and thereafter. Cholera outbreaks persisted to Fort Laramie and beyond, that is, at least seven hundred miles from the starting point. Beyond Fort Laramie cases decreased dramatically, and the disease seemed less virulent. Assuming a maximum distance of twenty miles per day, the emigrants would face at least five weeks under the threat of the disease.

Under the onslaught of cholera, some wagon trains simply disintegrated into separate isolated units. The daily repetition of sickness, suffering, death, and burial, burned terror into the hearts of many, and they drove on day and night in a furious blind attempt to flee from what they did not understand. Sick people were abandoned by the roadside, some not even suffering from cholera. The dying sometimes were avoided, and many of the dead were "buried" in graves that were no more than shallow holes. Some persons were interred who had not as yet died! On the other hand, if one stopped traveling because there was a cholera victim in his wagon, the possibilities increased that some or all the others who waited would eventually get the disease. That much seemed certain. Should the good of one be sacrificed for the good of all? Christian principles became pretty tattered, and experiences along the Platte River road were bitter and heart-rending as the fabric of friendship and family slowly dissolved.

Treatments prescribed for cholera victims were incredible, and more numerous by far than theories concerning its probable cause, but they accurately reflected medical thinking of the time. Doctors advised applying cloths steeped in warm water, or in spirits in which camphor had been dissolved, to the stomach; or else a warm poultice made of stewed garden mint; or a poultice made from mustard and strong vinegar. In addition, the patient was to be given a hot toddy.

Other doctors said that the error in most cholera treatment was in giving purgatives, with the object of "working off" the offending matter.

Rather, one grain of calomel with a teaspoonful of paregoric was to be administered; together, as one medical man advised, with "*ditto* of tincture of rhubarb, and *ditto* of compound tincture of cardamums in cold water, every three or four hours."

The *Cyclopaedia of Practical Medicine* published in 1845 recommended the use of opium, or opium and calomel. It was felt that these drugs had an excellent effect in allaying gastric and intestinal irritation, and, therefore "a grain of opium or a proportionate quantity of laudanum may be given every 2nd hour until relief is obtained." Diluent drinks in small quantities could be given, and "hot fomentations to the abdomen are well-calculated to afford relief, and the patient, if not too much exhausted, may remain for 15 minutes in a bath of 100°F., if obtainable. . . ."

As far back as 1832 Doctor Daniel Drake wrote a letter to the *Cincinnati Chronicle* (October 13, 1832) in which he recommended that cholera victims "take to bed, in a warm room and drink hot tea or sage, balm, or thorough wort, or even hot water. . . . Take a pouder of ten grains of Calomel and one of Opium mixed, if grown persons. . . ." Drake's advice was repeated by the writers of *The New London Medical, Pharmaceutical, & Posological Pocket Book* (1844):

To abate the irritation of the stomach at the onset, and to evacuate the acrid and redundant bile, the patient must be made to drink plentifully of diluent liquors, e.g., chicken broth (without salt), barley water, linseed tea, rice gruel, toast and water, etc., assisting the operation by means of tepid mucilaginous clysters of the same nature. . . . Opium, in the quantity of a grain to a grain and a half, with four or five grains of calomel, in the form of a pill, as soon as the stomach is sufficiently cleansed, repeated every two hours, or as long as the urgency of the case required. . . .

Blue pills or mercurial pills were prepared according to the 1830 *U.S. Pharmacopeia* as follows:

Take of purified mercury, and of confection of roses, each one ounce, liquorice root in powder, half an ounce; Rub the mercury with the confection in a glass mortar till the globules disappear; then add the liquorice and form a mass to be immediately divided into four hundred and eighty pills.

The doctors also bled, fed, starved, heated, purged, puked, shocked, injected, and steamed cholera sufferers, but nothing seemed to help. So the people died in the cities and they died on the plains, where the fumbling ministrations of family and friends, if not so learned and complex, were not any more or less futile. Numerous (and worthless) patent medicines soon became available for treatment of cholera, and perhaps the emigrants used such concoctions as "Forward's Cholera Drops" or "Brown's Cholera Mixture."

Today specific treatment for cholera recommends prompt parenteral therapy using adequate volumes of isotonic balanced electrolyte solutions to correct dehydration, acidosis, and hypokalemia. This treatment can lower the case fatality to less than 1 percent. Liquids containing glucose and saline are partially absorbed and are helpful when given by mouth. In other words, if the fluid balance is maintained, the cholera victim has a good chance of recovering. But this was not known on the plains, or in the cities, and so the victims died and were buried. Fathers, mothers, friends, relations, children, and old people died, leaving behind widows, widowers, orphans, and helpless individuals facing an uncertain and melancholy future.

There was little wood available on the prairie, so burial in coffins was out of the question. The dead were rolled or sewed in a blanket and placed in a hole. The latter might be lined with something or not, and if possible a board was placed over the body, which was then covered. The board was supposed to protect the corpse from the ravages of wolves and coyotes, but often it did not because the animals would burrow sideways to get at the body. Human bones, dismembered limbs, and clothing were found scattered over the plains. Indians also would disturb graves, but eventually some learned that this could have dire consequences. Markers were not always put up, for this would make the grave obvious. The mourners were torn between remembering the dead and singling the grave out for desecration. Many times the teams and horses would be run over the grave site to obliterate every trace of it and thus protect it from vandals; sometimes this worked, sometimes not— the wolves had a keen sense of smell. A Christian burial often meant a Christian ceremony of some kind at the graveside, but in their haste to flee, and with the increasing number of victims, this might be very brief, and the train would hurry on leaving behind a person or persons whose existence was now completely obliterated from the world. Burial was brief and secret. Because of the Indians a corpse might have to be carried in a wagon, and the stench often attracted large numbers of wolves.

There are a few grave markers still in existence, but most of them
have been stolen, or destroyed, or have deteriorated to meaningless
debris. While still fresh, though, some graves were strangely decorat-
ed. A.B. Hulbert noted:

Over the head of one was placed an inverted pair of hugh elk antlers.
They were full four feet high and formed an arch over the head of
the grave. A board bearing the name, age, and date of death of the
person who slept beneath was fastened across the horns.

Most often the markers consisted only of a plain board or piece
of wood on which the name, date, age, and home town of the victim
were crudely printed. There were only a few stone markers made, for
these required time and skill, as well as materials.

A great deal is said of death, dying, and burial in emigrant diaries, but details on childbirth are rare, even though births of a number
of trail babies were recorded.

The other intestinal ailments emigrants complained of were variously called diarrhoea, dysentery, inflammation of the bowels, or "colik." It has already been noted that chemical salts in the drinking water, particularly sodium sulfate, would have had a laxative effect likely
to be described as "diarrhoea." Poor diets and the tensions of the
journey, together with unsanitary arrangements for preserving left-
overs and for cleaning dishes and utensils, were factors in causing intestinal upsets. Typhoid fever is not mentioned often in the diaries
of emigrants; for being spared epidemics of this disease, they were
more fortunate than they realized.

Bacillary dysentery is characterized by a diarrhoea, often accompanied by chills and fever, and perhaps vomiting and stomach cramps.
It is spread by bacteria called *Shigella (S. dysenteriae, S. flexneri, S.
boydii, S. sonnei)*. They are fecal contaminants, and when an infected person transfers them to food, water, or eating utensils, susceptible
individuals can contract the disease by eating or drinking or using the
infected materials. It is, therefore, a disease that would flourish under
wagon train conditions. Bacterial dysentery is fortunately not a fatal
disease, and usually is self-limiting, but its effects are debilitating and
enervating to the victim.

There are a number of diarrhoeal diseases in which no specific
organism is implicated, but which are characterized by frequent and

purging fecal discharges leading to a generally weakened physical condition. Here again, the illness is self-limiting, and after one to three days the patient usually is on the way to recovery. General unsanitary conditions, and water and food heavily contaminated with bacteria transmitted via the fecal-oral route, are favorable for outbreaks of acute diarrhoea, especially in cramped quarters.

Since only a few wagon trains were ever fortunate enough to have a doctor traveling with them, treatments and medications were administered by whoever was available and willing to do the job. Perhaps in the case of dysentery and diarrhoea it was just as well not to have a doctor along, for if he had read the learned advice of *The Cyclopaedia of Practical Medicine,* and followed it, the patient would be administered calomel, and if necessary be bled with leeches "in the hepatic and praecordial region." No solid food was to be given, only barley water, rice gruel, or light broths. Dysentery also called for "small doses of *hydragyrum cum oreta* or calomel with Dover's powder, or the same mercurial preparations with opium and ipecacuan; lime water, vegetable astringents and bitters, as kino, catechua, cusparia, quassia, and logwood, nitric acid, balsam of copaiba or tolu; or various combinations. . . ." General bleeding was advised "at one week intervals," and "moderately stimulating and oleaginous frictions of the abdomen" were believed to be helpful.

The *Poor Man's Friend,* the popular home medical advisor of Dr. Gunn, however, suggested for dysentery or flux, "First, cleanse the stomach by an emetic or puke of ipecachuana; then give a purge of calomel; next, if the disease does not abate, you must repeat the purging daily with castor oil: this is the last medicine you can possibly use in this complaint." Then for good measure:

. . . give clysters frequently through the day made of slippery elm, which is to be thrown up the bowels cold. In the case of violent pain, bathe the stomach with laudanum, and spirits in which camphor has been dissolved, and apply cloths wrung out in hot water to the belly; or blister over the stomach. . . .

This was much too complicated to be adapted readily to trail conditions, so that in the end perhaps the treatment used for cholera calling for drinking a half-glass of the following concocted "medicine" every half-hour was more reasonable: "1 gallon of fourth proof West

India rum, one gallon of molasses, one quart of No. 6 [Thomson's lobelia, etc.] and 2 oz. cayenne pepper." Only three doses, however, were
to be used for prevention. Doctor Frisbee provided a recipe for "dysentery syrup," a bottle of which might easily be taken along on the road
west. This medicine was made as follows:

Take 2 oz. fir bark; 2 oz. black birch bark; 2 oz. popular bark, wormwood—1 handfull, all pounded fine; add 3 qts. water, boil for ½ hour
in a covered vessel; strain through a coarse cloth, add 3 lb. sugar to the
liquid, boil again until the scum has done rising; take the vessel from the
fire and add 1 oz. of cinnamon and 1 of cloves; stir them in, let stand
until cool—add 1 pt. of good brandy, stir, strain a second time and bottle.

One-half to one wine glass full was to be taken every two hours—until
relief was obtained, of course!

In 1848 George Catlin wrote of the Pawnees:

The present number of this tribe is ten to twelve thousand; about one
half the number they had in 1832, when that most appalling disease,
the small-pox, was accidentally introduced among them by Fur Traders,
and whiskey sellers; when ten thousand (or more) of them perished in
the course of a few months.

Smallpox decimated the Mandans, Assiniboins, Blackfeet, and others in the great epidemic of 1837. Luckily for the emigrants, they were
spared the ravages of this disease on the trail.

Ague, or malaria, followed its victims west. It was common in the
frontier communities, and numerous emigrants felt the cyclical rounds
of fever, chills, sweating, headache, and general lassitude that characterized it. Doctor J.C. Gunn suggested that in the "cold stage" (chills) one
should "take warm teas of any kind, provided they are weak, such as
sage, balm, hysop. . . . In many instances the Ague and the Fever can be
entirely cured by taking immediately from fifty to sixty drops of laudanum, with a few drops of peppermint, in warm tea. . . ." *The Families
New Guide to Health* advised, "take 10 grains of Calomel and 3 grams of
Tartar Emetic, this will act first as an emetic and then as a cathartic. If
no relief—use the steam bath—then give a 1 grain Quinine pill every hour
while there is no fever." A Doctor Hogg wrote that in the cold stage one
should bathe the feet in warm water, and in the hot stage one should
take cold, acidulated liquids; if there was a "congestion of the blood to

the head or delirium," leeches or cupping must be applied to the temples, and no opiates administered. During the time between stages, "give bark [quinine] and wine, and aromatics; if this occasions purging, give opiates, astringents; if costiveness, rhubarb." To all this Ware cautioned, "To every one who designs crossing the mountains we would earnestly say, avoid large quantities of medicines, pills, calomel, etc.—cleanliness and frequent bathing, are your best preventives of sickness. . . "

On the trail the malaria sufferer could do nothing but take to his wagon, "physik" himself as well as he could with blue pills, quinine, and powders, and hope to sleep off the attack. He might wish to take his quinine in Warburg's Drops. These consisted of cubebs, gentian, camphor, quinine, rhubarb, chalk, saffron, and aloes, all dissolved in alcohol. Dr. John Sappington included quinine in his Dr. John Sappington's Anti-Fever Pills first manufactured in 1832.

In early spring on the plains when it was rainy and cold, and the emigrants, not used to the strain of wagon travel, became fatigued and exhausted from overexposure and hard work, colds, sore throats, and bronchitis were rampant. These ailments made them even more miserable and despondent than the weather alone could. Superimposed on a nasty cold or swollen sore throat one might have various aches and pains induced by repeatedly pushing and hauling wagons out of mud sloughs, and over cold, swift-running streams, plus the possibility of a bad headache, a sick stomach, or traveler's diarrhoea, and the romantic picture of the happy, carefree emigrants imagined by some of the movies or on television is as false and misleading as their heroes' superhuman feats in defeating hordes of redskins singlehanded.

Here are a few cures for these ailments. Cough syrup: horehound —1 oz., thoroughwort—2 oz., juniper berries—½ pt., hyssop—1 handful, 2 tablespoons of flax seed; steep in 3 qts. of water until reduced to 3 pts., strain off and add 3 lb. sugar or 3 pts. molasses, and 2 oz. gum Arabic, steep again until reduced to 3 pts. This syrup is a laxative and tonic, and was considered to be an excellent remedy in coughs and colds, hoarseness and soreness of the lungs. A wine glass full could be taken three or four times a day. For a sore throat one could mix a pennyworth of pounded camphor in a wine glass of brandy, pour a small quantity of this on a lump of sugar, and allow to dissolve in the mouth every hour.

For inflammatory sore throat the Thomsonian view, as expressed in *The Families New Guide to Health,* was:

An emetic taken at a very early stage of this disorder will prevent it from forming. The next step is to give the steam bath... and a dose of Epsom salts with a fourth of a grain of Tartar Emetic in it. A mustard plaster, or a blister to the throat is an invaluable application. The diet should consist of barley or rice. The throat should be gargled with vinegar and water, inhaling the steam of hops in water from the spout of a teapot....

Folk remedies for colds and sore throats included tying a piece of peppered fat meat around the neck; grease from the Christmas goose; poultices made from mustard and onion; bloodroot or cherry bark; and rock candy in whiskey. Sol Tetherow, a wagon master on the Oregon Trail, prescribed for croup:

... boil the lickrish root to thick molasses. Take 1 fluid ounce, ½ ounce Balm Gilaid buds, 1 gil vinigar, 1 gil strong surup of skunk cabbage root, ½ fluid ounce tincter lobelia. Take a tea spoon full or so often as the case requires to keep the phlegm loos to rais easy.

Headaches could be eased by applying to the head a poultice made of, among other things, scraped raw potatoes. Cloths soaked in cold water, whiskey, and laudanum also were suggested as headache cures.

A mysterious disease was reported periodically by various emigrant groups, namely, "mountain fever." It was reported from the Platte River crossing to the Sacramento River. As the emigrants got to the thinner air, they encountered a prostrating seizure of nausea and violent headaches, frequently complicated with still another kind of dysentery; when the Mormons reached South Pass in 1847 they, too, encountered it. It was described as starting with a blinding headache, followed by severe pains in the back and joints, and accompanied by a high fever, often with delirium. The disease was not fatal, and the symptoms did not last for more than a few days. Various theories as to its cause were advanced. Some thought it was due to the day and night temperature variations in the mountains; others to the inhalation of alkali dust; or to the thin atmosphere; or to salts in the water; or to the milk. Later writers speculated that it might have been Rocky Mountain spotted fever. This disease is transmitted by the bite of a tick infected with the causa-

tive agent of the disease, *Rickettsia rickettsii.* The incubation period
varies from three to ten days, following which there is a sudden onset
of symptoms including a fever which may last from two to three weeks,
chills, and a macropapular rash that appears first on the arms and legs,
but later covers the entire body. The disease has a fatality rate of about
20 percent in untreated cases.

Colorado tick fever also is transmitted by the bite of a tick infected with a virus. This is an acute febrile disease that starts suddenly,
has a brief remission of fever, and then a second round, each lasting two
or three days. There is no rash produced. The victim may have an intense headache, and pains in the joints and muscles. The disease is
known to occur in the western regions of the United States and Canada,
and from the fragmentary descriptions available, it seems likely that
"mountain fever" was, in fact, Colorado tick fever. But there is no mention made of tick bites in emigrant diaries, to the best of my knowledge.
There is no specific treatment for this disease today, so any measures
the emigrants may have taken, besides lying in their wagons, were super-
fluous. Dr. Priddy Meeks of Salt Lake City advised mountain fever
victims to "jump all over in the City Creek, and crawl back into the tent
and cover up warm. . . . "

Before the advent of antiseptic surgery, lacerated wounds, compound fractures, and other traumatic accidents leading to exposed and
crushed muscle or bone were accompanied by septic infections, many
of which terminated fatally. Blood poisoning and gas gangrene were
common accompaniments of operations, and hospitals of the time were
regarded by many people as the gateways to horrible deaths. Amputations were performed under conditions that guaranteed massive infections, and the physical shock of such operations was almost insuperable.
A compound fracture of an arm or leg on the trail was an extremely serious matter because the consequences were always in doubt. Broken
bones could be set in a splint, of course, but if infection followed, and
amputation was required, and if no doctor was available, the emergency
procedures employed were almost certain to kill the patient. The only
anaesthetic was whiskey, and the only painkillers, opium and morphine.
The surgical instruments were butcher or hunting knives, and handsaws;
closing an artery on an amputated stump was done by searing it with a
red-hot iron, and although disinfectants such as quicklime, acids, and
chlorinated lime were known, whiskey was most commonly used. It is
no wonder that lacerated wounds or a compound fracture were looked

on with dread, and amputation of a limb was much preferred to treatment. Even the hospitals were deadly; between 1822 and 1850 of the 170 major amputations performed at the Massachusetts General Hospital, there was a mortality of 19 percent. Incredibly, Gunn's *Poor Man's Friend* devotes some pages to amateur amputation procedures including arm, thigh, leg, forearm, fingers, and toes!

Scurvy is caused by severe ascorbic acid (vitamin C) deficiency brought about by diets lacking in fresh fruits and vegetables. One pioneer wrote in his journal that scurvy ". . . made my lages acan [aching?], and swell and my mouth sore and gooms [gums] swell, and an acan pain all over." He and many of his fellow emigrants suffered from this disease in various stages of severity, but ironically, they probably could have alleviated the worst deficiency symptoms by tapping cacti or munching on the "weeds" that grew around them in the desert regions they passed through. It was known by 1601 that scurvy could be prevented by eating fresh fruits and vegetables, and by 1795 the British navy issued a daily lime juice ration to prevent this disease among the sailors. It is unfortunate that dried beans are poor in ascorbic acid, since this was the main source of it in the emigrants' diets.

In Doctor K. Imray's medical book written in 1849, there is a graphic description of scurvy, a disease met with in various stages of severity as the wagon trains neared their destinations in the West. He wrote that there is:

. . . general weakness, disinclination to move about, great lassitude after any ordinary bodily exercise, dull heavy pain in the back and limbs, great depression of spirits, disturbed sleep, weak and frequent pulse, loss of appetite, slow digestion, cold dry skin. . . gradually assumes a dingy, yellowish hue, the face looks puffed and bloated, the gums become swollen, dark, red-colored, or livid, spongy, and bleed from the slightest friction. As the disease advances the teeth loosen, the gums ulcerate, fungous excrescences shoot up from the ulcers and the breath acquires an exceedingly offensive smell. The urine also emits a peculiarly disagreeable rank odor, and appears muddy and highly colored. . . dark colored spots at the same time make their appearance on the calves of the legs, on the thighs, sometimes on the arms and back, rarely on the face; these run into one another, and form large blotches of a yellowish-greenish, or livid color, similar to marks which follow bruises or blows. . . . Ulcers in many cases form on the legs . . . the edges of the sore are a purplish color, and appear as inflated, a thin acrid foeted matter is at first discharged . . . the surface of the sore, under this dark bleeding mass, is soft, puffed, and spongy, and like the gums, bleeds from the slightest cause. As the disease gains ground, the knee-joints contract, the hams become swollen, hard, and painful. . . . In most cases the nostrils bleed occasionally. . . .

The onset of scurvy symptoms was slow and insidious. Coupled with the ever-increasing difficulties of the trail and its obstacles, and the cumulative decline of their strength engendered by weeks of exposure to sun, heat, thirst, dehydration, and back-breaking labor, the emigrants who suffered from scurvy were too weak and too resigned to view it other than as another result of their severe physical ordeal. The appearance of some scurvy sufferers became so alarming that they were ostracized by the others. This was especially true of the California-bound pioneers.

The last leg of the Overland Trail lay across the Nevada desert, along the Humboldt and Carson rivers. It was here that the challenge was most severe. Superimposed on everything else that had gone before, were heat exhaustion, thirst, dehydration, and sunstroke; all loomed large as likely to end the journey of man or animal. Here, in the shimmering heat, along somber, bitter, and sluggish rivers, in a barren country, among shallow graves, rotting carcases of oxen, mules, and horses, broken wagons and discarded paraphernalia, the tattered and near-prostrate emigrants slowly trudged under the watchful eyes of the buzzards. There was no natural shade, and some later wrote marveling that when they camped along the Carson River where some cottonwood trees were located, it was the first time in over 1,100 miles of traveling that they had encountered trees large enough to shade them. Mostly, the shadows of the wagons were the only protection against the searing sun.

When the water supply was short and had to be rationed, mothers gave their children sugar moistened with peppermint, or flattened bullets or spoons to suck on, just to keep saliva in their mouths. Even if a plentiful water supply was available, the animals were too spent to haul a large cargo of it—besides, the emigrants were not equipped to carry it.

After reaching the sink of the Humboldt River, the trail led either to the Truckee River or to the Carson River, and a stretch of desert had to be crossed, and then the Sierra Nevadas had to be climbed. All along the desert road the wayside was strewn with the dead bodies of oxen, mules, and horses, and the stench was horrible. The emigrants' traveling experiences had not prepared them for this. Many persons suffered greatly for water during the last 8 or 10 miles, and in many instances noble acts of generosity were seen. Some trains that got over before

Fig. 9   *The Rabbit Hole Springs.* Nevada scene along the
Humboldt River, as drawn in his diary by J. Golds-
borough Bruff. Reproduced by permission of the
Henry E. Huntington Library (HM 8044), San
Marino, California.

sent water back in kegs and left them on the road marked "for the benefit of the feeble."

Heatstroke results when the heat-regulating system of the body breaks down. Victims are generally those who exercise or work in excessive heat. They stop sweating and their body temperature rises, even, in some cases, to the point of inducing brain damage. Persons with heatstroke may be unaware that they have stopped sweating, and their body temperature may reach as high as 112°F. The skin is hot and dry, the pulse becomes weak, and a coma ensues.

In heat exhaustion or heat prostration, the syndrome is less severe than in heatstroke, but the sufferer becomes weak and dizzy, and falls down unconscious. Ordinarily, sweating continues and, in fact, the body temperature is slightly below normal. Along the Humboldt these effects were coupled with the added miseries of thirst. A dryness and tightness of the mouth and throat developed, later accompanied by tickling and burning sensations. The thirst-stricken body produces less saliva, the tongue may swell, the mouth and lips become progressively drier, and the whole organism begins to crave water. In severe cases the voice is lost, and the victim can only utter a hoarse whisper through parched and cracked lips.

In order to escape from the intense heat, some trains tried to cross the desert at night, or at least when the sun was going down. It was absolutely necessary that no breakdowns occur in the desert, because doing repairs there during the day was physically impossible.

Even when not in the desert, securing adequate water could be a problem, as Alonzo Delano related on a hot July day:

The afternoon was excessively warm, and the plain over which I was passing was destitute of water. I began to be thirsty. By degrees my mouth became dry and parched, and I experienced much torture. On the left, nearly a mile from the road, I saw a line of willows, which experience taught me was on the banks of a creek. Suffering intensely, I dragged myself to it, and found, alas! the bed perfectly dry. I could not find a single drop. My tongue began to swell; my mouth was dry, and I could scarcely articulate a word. I had often gone all day without water without much inconvenience, but now, for some reason, it seemed as if the very fountain of moisture was drying up. In this miserable state I dragged myself along for three miles farther, thinking I must use a last resort, when I caught sight of a cluster of willows growing near an outcrop of rock. With but small hope I went to it, and directly at the foot of the rock, a soft, miry spot showed indications of water. Stooping down, with my hands I scooped out the mud, and to my great delight water began to run in it. I could not wait for the mud to settle, but lay down to drink—faugh! The water was so strong of sulfur, that under any other circumstances, it would have made me vomit, but I drank enough to revive me, and then scooping the hole larger, I waited until it had settled, and then took a long hearty draught. Nauseous as it was, it appeared the most delightful draught I ever had.

There were numerous accidents among the emigrants as they drove their animals and wagons along the trail. Wheels crushed arms, legs, and sometimes bodies; mules kicked viciously and occasionally fatally; and there were frequent drownings at the ferries and fording places. Accidental gunshot wounds rated high on the list of the emigrants' woes. Numerous diarists remarked about incidents involving guns, and this is not surprising, since the emigrants generally were armed to the teeth with pistols and rifles, about which many of them knew very little. Some emigrants observed that more danger was to be apprehended from the carelessness with arms among their fellow emigrants than from hostile Indians.

There also were shooting accidents due to mistaken identities. One emigrant, M.B. Moorman, wrote in his diary on May 22, 1850:

At the last creek was a man lying wounded from a gunshot received in the following manner: He was out herding his cattle and when returning to camp mistook that of some other train for his own. He was hailed by the guard and his name demanded—he gave it, but the fiendish watch swore that he knew no such man and discharged his gun, the ball taking effect in his breast and ranged along the blade bone, inflicting a severe but not mortal wound. . . . "

Gun accidents involved such things as carelessly removing fully cocked rifles from wagons, carrying loaded and cocked guns in shirt pockets, mechanical defects, and general ignorance about the danger of firearms.

There was not much anyone on the trail could do for treating gunshot wounds. The primitive surgical conditions prevailing at the time made wounds of the body cavity almost hopeless even if a doctor was available. Bullets could be dug out of arms, legs, and thighs, but the shock attending this operation was likely to be great. Surgery was an extreme measure, and "disinfection" was limited to cleaning off the blood, and covering the wound with a bandage. The rest was left in the hands of God.

Drownings were common along the Missouri, Platte, and Green rivers. In attempting to swim stock over these and other rivers, emigrants often got entangled with their animals, and were pulled under in strong currents. The cold water also gave swimmers cramps, and in a dozen other ways many met, oddly enough, watery graves in the Great American Desert. Not one in a thousand could save his life by swimming, no matter how expert a swimmer. The water was cold, being formed from melted snows, and the current rolled and boiled and rushed with tremendous velocity. If a pioneer lost his footing, he was likely to be swept down by the current and drowned.

Ferries would capsize, throwing men, animals, and wagons into the swift rivers; bulging masses of rotted flesh in sodden homespun were seen downstream looking very much like water-soaked tree trunks.

Numerous accidents occurred on the trail in which the animals and wagons were involved. In easing loaded wagons down steep inclines, such as the one at Ash Hollow, each vehicle had to be brought down separately. The rear wheels sometimes were locked with chains and the wagons held back with ropes. If these frayed and parted, the wagon might roll uncontrolled down the hill, smashing up at the bottom and scattering driver and contents everywhere. If necessary, oxen were hitched to the rear of the wagons, and as they pulled up the hill, they acted as an additional brake to the wagon's descent. Of course, all goods in the wagon had to be lashed down.

A.J. Delano related in his diary for May 25, 1849, "During the day we passed a poor fellow who had fallen from his wagon, which passed over him, breaking his leg in two places. . . ." More pathetic than these accidents to drivers, however, were those involving children falling from jostling or stampeded wagons, and being crushed under the wheels. An Oregon pioneer of 1843, J.W. Nesmith,[1] made this entry for Thursday, July 20:

. . . came up to a fresh grave with stones piled over it, and a note tied on a stick, informing us that it was the grave of Joel Hembree, child of Joel J. Hembree, aged six years, and was killed by a wagon running over its body. At the head of the grave stood a stone containing the name of the child, the first death that occurred on the expedition.

---

[1] J. W. Nesmith, "Diary of the Emigration of 1843," *Oregon Historical Quarterly* 7 (1906): 341–42.

There were many more destined to follow little Joel in the years to come.

The animals themselves, especially the mules, were the cause of numerous accidents. E.D. Perkins, for example, told in his diary entry for Friday, August 31, 1849:

> . . . I noticed that the pack of one of my mules, little "Vic" was loose & I stopped her, tightened it and whistled her to go again when she passed me she gave me a severe kick on the hip with both her hind feet laming me considerably. . . . Not more than an hour afterward I punished her, I stopped her again to arrange her pack which seemed unusually troublesome, & as before had turned her loose when she suddenly wheeled so as to bring her artillery to bear upon me, & let fly with all her strength striking me full in the breast one of them breaking my watch crystal into a hundred pieces & injuring the watch itself, & the force of the blow knocking me backwards down the hill side heels over head.

Occasionally there would be a stampede. Something would trigger off the animals in a train. Perhaps a rattlesnake, or a lightning flash, or a clap of thunder, or the smell of distant water, and in an instant the animals were off on a frantic, crazed run in a careening race across the plains. The drivers could only hope to keep their wagons upright, and to avoid any holes or obstacles that would destroy both the wagon and its contents and perhaps kill or seriously injure any occupants. Eventually things would be brought under control, and the panting animals halted. Behind them might be the litter of broken wagons, scattered belongings, injured and dying animals, and sometimes broken people as well. In a minute the possessions and means of travel of an entire family might be wiped out, and these unfortunates then had to depend entirely on their fellow emigrants for assistance, until (hopefully) their wagon could be repaired and new animals procured—a doubtful hope at best.

After months of traveling under daily stress, some of the emigrants began to show signs of folding under their burdens. Daily tensions built up into inevitable explosions, and diarists record numerous outbreaks of dissension among emigrants, as they began to suffer a sort of "trail fatigue" that no amount of resting would alleviate. Pioneer Pritchard wrote in his diary for May 23, 1849:

> . . . an unfortunate difficulty. . . took place between Charles Hodges & P.S. Hamline, last evening whilst they were engaged in their culinary operations. Some unpleasant words passed whereupon Hodges struck Ham-

line & Knocked him down—and was beating him sevearly. When the cry
of fight was given, I was the first who got there and pulled Hodges off
Hamline—when Knives and Pistols were drawn. I caught Hamline just
in the act of stabing Hodges with a large Bouy-Knife, and in the effort
to arest the stroke I received a slight cut myself about one and a half
inches long across my right arm.

Now and then a murder occurred, and most of the time the mur-
derer escaped. Where did he go? How did he live? These are unan-
swered questions. It is assumed that the villain probably joined some other
wagon train, presumably telling them a hard luck story of some sort.
Sometimes the murderers were caught, and after a very brief "trial"
were hung on the spot.

Hulbert related the story of a woman whose husband refused her
wish to go back home. As a consequence of his refusal she began trying
to set fire to their wagon, and after several failures succeeded in destroying all their belongings. Such individuals, Hulbert wrote, ". . . were de-
mented . . . [their] minds had given way through fear, worry, or lone-
someness, or because of poor food or water, overwork, sleeplessness,
disease, or family disputes, or all or any of these combined." Diarists
tell of lifelong partnerships and friendships dissolved over trivial differences; of emigrants losing their minds and having to be tied down in
their wagons, and, of course, there were the inevitable suicides. Along
the Humboldt River, where intense and continuous pressure was placed
on the emigrants, suicides commonly occurred, and a diarist noted that
on one day, "three men and two women drowned themselves."

Among the various expeditions to the West in the forties, three
typify some of the serious problems encountered by emigrants; these
are the St. Joseph's Company led by Stephen Meek in 1845; the Donner
Party to California in 1846; and the Sand Walking Company of 1849.

Approximately 246 wagons left for Oregon from the banks of the
Missouri River in the spring of 1845. At Fort Hall 46 wagons departed
for California for various reasons, and the others faced the rough trail
along the Snake River and across the Blue Mountains to the Columbia
River. Stephen Meek, perhaps induced by Elijah White into attempting
to find a route that would save two hundred miles or more of travel, led
about two hundred families comprising the St. Joseph's Company across
a trail thereafter called Meek's Cut-off. They started on an old path
that trappers and hunters had used, following it along the Malheur River. This road was rough and difficult, the oxen soon became foot sore

and worn out, and Meek, it turned out, was not familiar with the route, although he was to be paid three hundred dollars for his services as a guide. The party turned south but ran into the desert; they then turned north to where the headwaters of the Columbia ought to have been, but found nothing. Their food supplies became exhausted, and some of the emigrants died. It was thought they had "camp fever" (probably moun- tain fever), but there also was dysentery among them. They came to a marshy lake and were unsuccessful in attempts to cross it. Since the marsh appeared to bear south, and the emigrants were low on provisions, they still were determined to go north, and would not follow Meek, who advised them the other way. Proceeding along a dry ridge between the Deschutes and John Day rivers, the emigrants spent their time in look- ing for springs and pursuing their thirst-crazed cattle. There were only dead-ends among the rocky canyons, and after 2 weeks they became even more desperate as well as more distraught with Meek. Feeling his life was in danger, Meek and his wife fled in the direction of The Dalles. Subsequently 9 men were detached from the party; they headed in what they hoped was the direction of The Dalles, with only four days provi- sions. Nine days later they reached The Dalles, suffering from hunger and exhaustion. At the mission the Reverend Waller furnished the men with food, and it was there that they met a mountaineer named Black Harris, who agreed to return with them to find the rest of the St. Jo- seph's Company. Twenty days later the main party was located and found to be in great difficulty—lacking both sufficient food and water, and suffering from disease. Many graves marked the emigrants' road, but they finally reached The Dalles via Meek's Cut-off about six weeks after they had started. In the *Missouri Republican* (St. Louis, July 17, 1846) there was an account of this event that read in part,

Mr. Smith gives a most meloncholy [sic] account of the progress and suf- ferings of the St. Joseph's company of emigrants, which left in 1845, un- der the pilotage of Mr. Meek. This company lost their way and endured incredible hardships. They were out forty days longer than usual, and before their arrival at The Dalles of the Columbia, some seventy-five of the company had died.

The story of the Donner party has been told numerous times; it a classic of courage, cowardice, and suffering among early western pio- neers. It began by a desire to save time, and a promise by Lansford W. Hastings that his cut-off from Fort Bridger over the Wasatch Mountains

to Salt Lake City, across the Great Salt Lake Desert, and thence between, over, and around various mountain ranges, meeting the trail on
the Humboldt River, would, in fact, be just that. From Fort Bridger
the trail normally led along Muddy Creek and the Bear River valley to
Soda Springs, and thence to Fort Hall. It followed the Snake River and
just beyond American Falls turned southwest along the Raft River to
City of Rocks.

Following the Hastings Cut-off, the eighty (!) miles across the desert
was an unexpected and critical challenge to the Donner Party. They had
just spent an exhausting three weeks chopping, shoveling, and struggling with their wagons over the Wasatch Mountains, and the desert experience superimposed on this was the last straw, although they did not
realize it. The "cut-off" itself turned out to be 125 miles longer than
the regular route.

Along the way to the Sierra Nevadas, there were several murders,
Indian attacks, and almost unbearable suffering from heat and thirst.
Wagons and equipment were abandoned, animals strayed and died, and
the party's progress became ever slower. They lost their race with time.

In mid-October the Donner Party camped on the Truckee River,
and toward the end of the month they were on their way to Truckee
(now Donner) Lake. The first heavy snowfall in the mountains had occurred, and that was the herald of doom for them—they would be hopelessly snowbound and facing starvation until the following March. They
had arrived too late to cross the mountains, and now would pay a terrible price for the time wasted by taking Hastings's advice. Several heroic
attempts to rescue the party were made after news of their condition
was brought to Sutter's Fort and Yerba Buena, but the relief parties
had little success, and during the long nightmare of winter, starvation,
exposure, and exhaustion took a steady toll of lives. Finally the surviv-
ors were forced to resort to cannibalism in order to keep themselves alive. Two persons were killed to be eaten; these were Indians sent over
from Sutter's as part of a rescue operation that failed. For the most
part, those who died in camp were preserved by the extreme cold, and
it was they who were eaten. Forty-two persons out of the eighty that
started from Illinois survived to reach California.

In the spring of 1847 Captain Jefferson Hunt and some members
of the Mormon Battalion were taking John C. Frémont back from Mon-
terey to Fort Leavenworth for court-martial when they came upon the

grisly remains of the Donner camp. Bodies and parts of bodies were still scattered around; Captain Hunt's party stayed long enough to bury most of the remains. Some of the miserable cabins of the Donner camp remained for several years after the tragedy, and together with a few bones marked the site of this most famous trail tragedy. The episode had effects on later emigrations; more specifically, it spelled the end of the Hastings Cut-off, and it led to opening the more northerly Lawson route to California, with the abandonment of the Truckee route. Eventually Truckee Lake became Donner Lake, and since that time the Donner Party and their tragic fate have been remembered by place names such as Donner Pass, Donner Creek, and Donner Peak.

Manley[2] has described the ordeal of the Sand Walking Company in his book *Death Valley in '49*. In emigrant camps at Salt Lake City an organization called the Sand Walking Company was established for the purpose of taking a southern route to Los Angeles and thence to the gold mines. It was a large group, consisting of 200 people, 107 wagons, and over 500 cattle and horses, and they left the Salt Lake settlement in October, 1849. Around November 1 the company encountered a Captain Smith, who showed them a map prepared by Colonel Williams that revealed a shorter westward route than the one their leader, Captain Jefferson Hunt, was taking. Dissension followed, most emigrants wishing to follow Smith, only seven wagons going on with Hunt even though he was a veteran of numerous trips to California. After a while, however, it became apparent that Smith's notions of a shortcut were wrong, and more than sixty wagons rejoined Hunt's party, except for the group of Asabel Bennett, with which Manley was associated, and another group of young men calling themselves the Jayhawkers.

Scouts thought they had found a way west through the canyons, and twenty-seven wagons committed themselves to what was to be the first walk by white men across the Death Valley region. Twenty of the wagons belonged to the Jayhawkers, and as they all were young men in a great hurry to reach the California gold fields, it was decided to go on ahead of the other seven wagons encumbered with women and children. Those left behind formed what was called the Bennett-Arcane party, and Manley served as their scout. The party consisted of Mr. and Mrs.

---

2   W. L. Manley, *Death Valley in '49,* American Facsimile Series No. 90 (Ann Arbor: University Microfilms, 1966). This was originally published in 1894— forty-five years after the events took place.

Asabel Bennett and three children; Mr. and Mrs. J. B. Arcane and son; Mr. and Mrs. Wade and three children; two Earhart brothers and their sons; Captain Culverwell; John Rogers, a man named Fish, another named Gould, and four unnamed teamsters—a total of fourteen men, nine children, and three women. They decided not to try to follow the Jayhawkers, but rather to go their own way. Eventually the Jayhawkers returned, their dreams of a short northern route across the mountains having been shattered. Soon the emigrants and their animals began to suffer for lack of water as they trudged over the sere desert lands, and it was clear that they had to find a pass through the mountains to California or die. After terrible physical hardships Manley and Rogers, who had gone on ahead, managed to scale the Panamint and San Gabriel mountains, as well as to cross the Mojave Desert and arrive in the San Fernando Valley. After resting and securing some supplies, they quickly had to return to the desert and guide out the rest of the party, so their sufferings began anew. Eventually most of the group reached California after a desert trip of 1,700 miles. The Jayhawkers had broken up and were scattered, but most of them finally came struggling into California.

In February of 1846 the Mormons fled Nauvoo to escape religious persecution, and crossed the icy Mississippi River into Iowa. As they moved west, locating themselves at Sugar Creek, Garden Grove, Mt. Pisgah, and then Kanesville, they suffered all manner of hardships and diseases including exposure to cold and freezing weather, lack of food, dysentery, ague, scurvy, croup, sore throats, and whooping cough. In August of 1846 they established their winter quarters on the Missouri River at the site of modern Florence, Nebraska. The Pioneer Company, led by Brigham Young, started out in April of 1847 to seek a new home in the West. It has been said that this trek must have been the most extensively reported emigration in history, since at least fifteen persons kept some kind of journal or diary, many of which were later published. The Mormon emigrants traveled on the north side of the Platte River, sometimes called the Mormon Trail, via South Pass to Fort Bridger, and thence through Echo, Weber, and East canyons, and over the Wasatch Mountains to the Salt Lake valley. There was not much novelty in this route, but it was the road over which emigration of an *entire* group of people occurred. The Big Company of emigrants followed the Pioneer Company, after Brigham Young had declared that "this is the place," and by October 2, 1847, the bulk of the Mormon population had traveled 1,032 miles from Winter Quarters to Salt Lake City. Their sufferings were relatively light, and although there were some accidents and difficulties encountered, only seven deaths were reported. But the later "handcart brigades" of emigrating Mormons of the 1850s suffered severely while on the trail. The real suffering of the Mormons of the forties occurred before they left Winter Quarters.

The Indians, aside from stealing horses and firearms, gave the emigrants relatively little difficulty. Along the trail they might have met with Pawnees, Sioux, Omahas, Crows, Shoshones, Utes, Snakes, Nez Percé, Blackfeet, Cayuses, and Diggers, but it was the last along the Humboldt River who caused the most trouble.

The Diggers had arrows tipped with glass or iron, which they shot from short bows. They were said to be able to shoot an arrow through a man's body, and many oxen along the Humboldt were severely wounded by powerfully propelled Digger arrows. Any arrow wound was serious, because of the likelihood of infection. The only thing the pioneers could do was to pull out the arrow and cauterize the wound with a red-hot iron, or "disinfect" it in some way and cover it with a clean bandage. If the arrow had to be dug out of the flesh, the situation was about the same as it would be for a gunshot wound.

There was little of whooping Indians astride fast ponies encircling a beleaguered wagon train and shooting arrows into it in the forties, Frontal attacks were rare, and the Indian was not so stupid as to attempt one. There were some ambush attempts but, in general, the Indian was not the white man's main concern; as it turned out, the white man was to become the Indians' bête noire and ultimate destroyer.

7

THE GREEN AND GOLDEN LANDS

Most of those who had walked over two thousand miles of deserts and mountains and plains found themselves in either the Willamette, Sacramento, or San Joaquin valleys. If they were farmers, a whole growing year had been lost, and probably the profits from yet another were invested to finance the journey. Now that they had arrived at last in the green and golden lands of Oregon and California, one might ask whether it was worth the trouble.

There is no doubt that the attractions of California and Oregon had been heavily publicized. The salubrious climate, the fertile soil, the natural mineral wealth, and the excellent harbors of California were coupled to a thin population of weak, lazy, and pleasure-loving Mexicans. Economically and politically, it seemed natural that California should become part of the United States and it was destined to do so soon. Antoine Robideaux in 1840 described California as a land of sunshine and fertility, teaming with horses, cattle, and oranges. By the midforties there was a vigorous California emigration campaign in progress, but after the discovery of gold in 1848 no further efforts to lure people to California were needed. According to the California State Mining Bureau, the value of gold mined in 1849 was $10 million; in 1850, $41 million; in 1851, $76 million; and in 1852, $81 million.

As far as Oregon was concerned, in his book *Astoria* Washington Irving wrote:

A remarkable fact, characteristic of the country west of the Rocky Mountains, is the mildness and equability of the climate. . . the rigorous winters and sultry summers, and all the capricious inequalities of temperature prevalent on the Atlantic side of the mountains, are but little felt on their western declivities. The countries between them and the Pacific are blessed with milder and steadier temperature, resembling the climate of parallel latitudes in Europe. In the plains and valleys but little snow falls throughout the winter, and usually melts while falling. . . . The . . . year, from the middle of March to the middle of October, an interval of seven months, is serene and delightful.

But all was not wine and roses for Oregon, and one emigrant was not enchanted when he said:

. . . water is so very scarce, that it [the Columbia plain] can never be generally fed; unless indeed, as some travelers in their praises of this region seem to suppose, the animals that usually live by eating and drinking, should be able to dispense with the latter, in a climate where nine months in the year, not a particle of rain or dew falls, to moisten a soil as dry and loose as a heap of ashes.

The emigrant was of the opinion that between the Cascade range and the Blue Mountains there were only a few livable areas in a series of deserts, and that, in general, Oregon was mostly a sterile land.

Nevertheless, the Reverend H.H. Spaulding felt that Oregon had "great possibilities" for raising livestock, and he was particularly impressed with the farming opportunities of the valleys along rivers such as the Willamette, Deschutes, John Day, Umatilla, and Walla Walla. So it was that through 1848 more emigrants headed for Oregon than for California (even more emigrants went to Utah in the great Mormon migration of 1847–48), and it is not surprising that most of them headed for the Willamette valley and Fort Vancouver. In actual fact, however, the total number of Oregon immigrants up to 1850 was not very large.

The emigrants to Utah and Oregon had come to stay, but those who headed for California directly after the gold discovery generally were males of a less settled state of mind. Many expected to pick up a fortune in California and then go back to civilization in the East; some did, but many did not. It has been said that Forty-Nine was a "put-on," and that, for the most part, the money spent in traveling to the mines and in buying prospecting gear could have been better invested back home.

What physical condition were the emigrants in when they finally arrived at their Pacific paradise? Many of them were completely worn out and exhausted by the long months of travel. They needed a rest, relaxation and some good food. They were suffering from fatigue, malnutrition, and the cumulative effects of poor diets, as well as from their exposure to the rain, heat, and cold. A number of them probably had incipient scurvy and chronic diarrhoea or intestinal troubles. Months of living under poor hygienic conditions also had left their mark. Emigrants had numerous skin, hair, teeth, and eye problems. Focal infections were exacerbated, and such annoyances as eczema, cracked fingers and lips, open sores, scalp disorders, rotting teeth, eyes reddened and weakened by sun and glare probably were common. Some had respiratory problems caused by the constant inhalation of alkali dust. Those who had become sick en route had little chance to convalesce properly under conditions like those existing along the Humboldt or Snake rivers, or over the Sierra Nevada or Blue Mountains. Sometimes the sick merely became the "walking sick," and had to struggle to keep up with the others. But many of these would bear scars of the trail for the rest of their lives. Those who were seriously ill for some time, and, as a consequence, "took their medicine," probably ended up with mercury poisoning of varying degrees of severity, or with an addiction to opium, or both!

The psychological effects of the journey must have been long lasting, especially if one had encountered and survived some deadly hazard like a stampede, or a rattlesnake bite, or a gunshot wound, or near drowning. There was plenty of death to see in the cholera epidemics of 1849 and thereafter. The ordeal of the trail in the forties lay in its incessant demands for work and vigilance, and the consequent worry and pressure these imposed on men and women alike. Their experiences permanently colored attitudes toward domestic life in the new surroundings. Some may have found any further adjustments too difficult to make. It should be remembered, however, that some pioneers were used to moving, first having come from the East to settle in Illinois, Wisconsin, or Missouri. But few of them had experienced "the Elephant" before; that much is certain.

The romanticized picture of happy pioneer families quickly settling down in their new locations in the trans-Mississippi West seems much overdrawn. Most emigrants arrived at their destinations as a poor and sickly lot; they badly needed a period of freedom from toil. Their hopes lay as much in their children's fresh opportunities as for themselves. It was to be a young person's world. The new settlers got no rest. They had to build homes, plow fields, set up their business, plant crops, and try to keep their weary bodies going. They viewed life pragmatically, like the farmers and shopkeepers they were, in terms of returns for effort invested. They soon learned that the promises of the land were not going to be fulfilled quickly, and that years of labor would be necessary before their dreams became realities. That was what the future held for most of them, and for most of them, it was enough. Life on the trail was finished, and a new one had begun.

The first few weeks after reaching the end of the trail were hard, very hard for some families. Hastings, in his *Emigrant's Guide to Oregon and California* (1845) wrote: "A kindness exists among those pioneers of the west, which is almost unparalleled. Upon arrival of emigrants, in the country, immediate arrangements are made by former settlers, to provide them with houses and provisions, and every aid is rendered in making their selection of lands and procuring houses for themselves. ... " One could not always count on this, and after five months the battered and decaying wagons would still be "home," at least for a few more weeks. Arriving in the Oregon Territory, perhaps somewhere in the fertile Willamette valley, the immigrant might find the number of jobs that had to be done before settling down endless. Woods had to be cleared, logs cut to make a cabin, a source of water had to be found, new clothing made, food procured, and all this and more to be done before winter set in.

Most log cabins were not very large, usually around twenty by thirty feet. All were built with a fireplace—an absolute essential for a pioneer dwelling. The fireplace was a source of heat and light, and the only means for cooking. A fair fireplace and chimney could be built, if done carefully, with heavy sticks plastered with clay both inside and outside. Later on a stone fireplace could be made. There were no windows in early log cabins, just apertures cut in the walls, but some fancier ones used small sliding panels which could be opened in good weather. Glass, of course, was unavailable. The cabin was kitchen, bedroom, and living room combined, although some Missouri pioneers erected what they called a "dog-trot" cabin. This consisted of two identical cabins separated by a cabin length, over which a common roof was built. One of the cabins served as a kitchen and dining area while the other was used as a bedroom. The open space could be used for outdoor activities during nice weather.

There was little in the way of furnishings, and what there was generally consisted of rude beds, chairs, and a table, all made from the wood of cedar trees. Later on, when the sawmills came in, better wood for cabins and more comfortable furniture became available; but the first settlers had to depend upon themselves.

Food was not too much of a problem, and fish, game, and berries were available for the taking. The ingenious pioneer housewife was equal to preparing meals from practically anything at hand. In the same way she was able to make clothes, and indeed, the canvas of old wagon covers often was lined with remnants of old clothing to make warm windbreakers and raincoats.

The new West was not only expensive to reach, but expensive to live in. Everything was in short supply. In 1850 a single room in Oregon City might cost anywhere from $25 to $75 a month. Flour was $15 a barrel. Newspapers and magazines, as well as mail, were practically nonexistent. It took time and money for a midwestern hog and corn farmer to learn how to grow fruit and vegetables. In a semidry area the cost of farming was bound to be high, and the need for machinery, labor ($2 a day for a white man, $1 a day for an Indian, and $10 a month for a woman), water rights, and land itself, gradually rose. Cash was scarce, and many business transactions were carried out by bartering. Eggs, butter, bacon, oats, hay, etc., often were coin of the realm.

The settlers spread out—they wanted farmland not city neighbors —and Oregon City had only sixty-two buildings after its first year and a half of existence. You could get lonely and depressed in a place far removed from anyone but your family—nothing in sight but work, and more work.

In California, after the discovery of gold, the somewhat dormant pastoral economy leaped forward, with emphasis on industry and commerce. Agricultural pursuits declined as practically everyone rushed to the gold mines to make his fortune. This exodus from the farm produced the curious result that the demand for agricultural produce soon outstripped the supply, and indeed so spectacular was this development that it became extremely profitable to become a farmer again. In addition, the cattle market soared as demands for beef became insatiable.

So the vast farmlands and large herds slowly developed from small beginnings. The pioneers prospered and finally had time to help those who followed. They had conquered the West and made it into their own American image, a new society modeled on the old, but more to their liking. It was the beginning of the end for the frontier, but it would always remain a land of hope and promise for those seeking a fresh start in life.

REFERENCES

A number of original diaries and letters written in the forties were read in the preparation of this work. I have sought a representative rather than exhaustive coverage of them. In addition, there is a vast literature including published diaries of trans-Mississippi emigrants, and this has not been ignored. But diaries written during overland journeys tended to be irregular and laconic. Many emigrants were barely literate, and others were often too exhausted after an arduous day to scribble anything more than a line or two, if even that much. Day-by-day reports do not generally read like epics. Letters written to those back home are longer and more detailed, but harder to come by. In many cases I have incorporated the "sense" of an episode into the narrative without specifically quoting the source.

Time's hand over a span of 130 years or more has left many diaries faded, brittle, and ever less accessible. In many accounts, whatever their source or form, some details were probably either omitted, added, or embellished, accidentally or purposely—we will never really know. "Reminiscences" are suspect, and one wonders how accurate the memory can be when, for example, one tries to recall events a quarter of a century or more removed, as some writers did.

I am grateful for the assistance rendered by many librarians and curators throughout the country. My special thanks go to Mrs. Gordon E. Gatherum of the Ohio Historical Society, Mrs. Nancy C. Prewitt of the University of Missouri Library and the Western Historical Manuscript

Collection, Mr. Jay Williar of the California Historical Society, Mr. J.D. Cleaver of the Oregon Historical Society, Mr. James E. Potter of the Nebraska State Historical Society, Miss Lida Lisle Green of the Iowa State Department of History, Mrs. Dorothy Hanks and Dr. John Blake, both of the National Library of Medicine, and to Col. J.H. Henderson of the Armed Forces Medical Museum. My thanks also are expressed to the University of Maryland General Research Board for a travel grant that enabled me to visit the libraries referred to here.

This book does not pretend to be a scholarly work, nor was it intended primarily for scholars, although some historians may find useful material in it. I have addressed myself primarily to the general reader and those interested in nineteenth-century western Americana, and to this end, the following brief list of references for further reading and information on particular facets of emigrant life is offered.

Anderson, M.H. (ed.). *Appleton Milo Harmon Goes West.* Berkeley: Gillick, 1946.

Billington, R.A. *The Far Western Frontier.* New York: Harper & Row, 1956.

Clark, T.D. (ed.). *Gold Rush Diary: Being the Journal of Elisha Douglas Perkins on the Overland Trail in the Spring and Summer of 1849.* Lexington: University of Kentucky Press, 1967.

Coy, O.C. *The Great Trek.* Los Angeles: Powell, 1931.

Dale, H.C. (ed.). *The Ashley-Smith Explorations and the Discovery of a Central Route to the Pacific, 1822–1829.* Glendale, Calif.; Clark, 1941.

Delano, A.J. *Life on the Plains and among the Diggings* (1854). March of America Facsimile Series No. 89. Ann Arbor: University Microfilms, 1966.

DeVoto, B. *Across the Wide Missouri.* Boston: Houghton Mifflin, 1947.

Dick, E. *The Sod House Frontier: 1854–1890.* New York: Appleton, 1937.

Driggs, H.R. *Westward America.* New York: Putnam, 1942.

Dryden, C.P. *Give All to Oregon!* New York: Hastings House, 1968.

Dunlop, R. *Doctors of the American Frontier.* New York: Doubleday, 1965.

Ghent, W.J. *The Road to Oregon* (1929). New York: AMS, 1970.

Gilbert, E.W. *The Exploration of Western America, 1800–1850.* Cambridge: Cambridge University Press, 1933.

Hollin, W. E. *The Great American Desert*. New York: Oxford University Press, 1966.

Hulbert, A. B. *The Forty-Niners: The Chronicle of the California Trail*. Boston: Little, Brown, 1931.

Jones, B. M. *Health Seekers in the Southwest, 1817-1900*. Norman: University of Oklahoma Press, 1967.

Mattes, M. J. *The Great Platte River Road*. Nebraska State Historical Society, publication 25, Lincoln: 1969.

Miller, T. *The Birth of Modern America: 1820-1850*. New York: Pegasus, 1970.

Morgan, D. L. (ed.). *The Overland Diary of James A. Pritchard from Kentucky to California in 1849*. Denver: Old West, 1959.

Paden, I. D. *The Wake of the Prairie Schooner*. New York: Macmillan, 1944.

——.(ed.). *The Journal of Madison Berryman Moorman* (1850). San Francisco: California Historical Society, 1948.

Parkman, F. *The Oregon Trail* (1849). New York: Signet Classics, 1962.

Pickard, M. E., and Buley, R. C. *The Midwest Pioneer: His Ills, Cures and Doctors*. New York: Schuman, 1946.

Read, G. W., and Gaines, R. (eds.). *Gold Rush: The Journals, Drawings and Other Papers of J[oseph] Goldsborough Bruff* (1849). New York: Columbia University Press, 1949.

Riegel, R. *America Moves West*. New York: Holt, 1930.

——. *Young America*. Norman: University of Oklahoma Press, 1949.

Rosenberg, C. E. *The Cholera Years*. Chicago: University of Chicago Press, 1962.

Shryock, R. H. *Medicine and Society in America*. New York: New York University Press, 1960.

Steckmesser, K. L. *The Westward Movement*. New York: McGraw-Hill, 1969.

Stegner, W. *The Gathering of Zion*. New York: McGraw-Hill, 1964.

Stewart, G. R. *Ordeal by Hunger*. Boston: Houghton Mifflin, 1936; rev, 1960.

——. *The California Trail*. New York: McGraw-Hill, 1962.

Stone, I. *Men to Match My Mountains*. New York: Doubleday, 1956.

Among the manuscripts and letters written through 1849, those listed here are from the Overland Journeys to the Pacific Manuscript

Collection (No. 1508) of the Oregon Historical Society, and were consulted by the author: Bayley, B., letter, 1845; Beal, J., account, 1847; Bone, G. L., 1848; Caulfield, R., letter, 1848; Harrison, J. M., account, 1846; Harty, J. M., letter, 1847; Hill, A. and S., account, 1843; King, S. and M., 1846; McKinney, N., 1845; Morfitt, W., reminiscences, 1847; Parker, S., diary, 1845; Reynor, J., 1847; and Stillwell, W. D., 1844.

Other manuscripts of the Oregon Historical Society not in the above collection that were read include: MS 520-Field, J., diary, 1845; MS 697-Garrison, M. E. R., reminiscences, 1845; MS 41-Geer, E. S., account, 1847; MS 11-Harden, A. B., diary, 1847, letters 1848; MS 947-Harritt, J., diary, 1845; MS 660-Hastings, L. B., journal, 1847; MS 659-Howells, J. E., journal, 1845; MS 722-Lyman, H. S., reminiscences of J. T. Cox, 1846; MS 543-McHaley, G. W., journal, 1843; MS 1072-Pattison, W., diary, 1849.

The following accounts of overland journeys were consulted at the California Historical Society: Bowers, F. M., 1845; Brown, J. E., memoirs, 1849; Cutler, E. C., papers, 1849; Decker, P., diary, 1849; Dwindle, J. W., 1849; Hixson, J. M., 1849; Kimball, W., 1849; McIlhany, E. C., recollections, 1849; and McWilliams, J., recollections, 1849.

D. L. Morgan in *The Overland Diary of James A. Pritchard* has referenced every known diary kept in 1849 on the South Pass route to California, Utah, and Oregon as of 1959. In addition, M. Mattes in *The Great Platte River Road* has included a comprehensive bibliographic listing of hundreds of overland narratives.

Many accounts written in 1850 or thereafter, as well as reprinted accounts through 1849, also were referred to during the course of this work. Among the latter were:

Applegate, J., *Oregon Historical Quarterly* 1 (1900): 371-83.

Arthur, J., *Transactions of the Oregon Pioneer Association* (1887): 96-104.

Berrien, J. W., *Indiana Magazine of History* 56 (1960): 273-352.

Boardman, J., *Utah Historical Quarterly* 2 (1929): 99-121.

Bonney, B. F., *Oreg. Hist. Quart.* 24 (1923): 36-55.

Buck, W. W. *Trans. Oreg. Pioneer Assn.* (1894): 67-69.

Case, W. M., *Oreg. Hist. Quart.* 1 (1900): 269-77.

Clark, B. C., *Missouri Historical Review* 23 (1928): 3-43.

Collins, M. E. G., *Oreg. Hist. Quart.* 17 (1916): 358-72.

Cosgrove, H., *Oreg. Hist. Quart.* 1 (1900): 253-96.

Deady, M. P., *Trans. Oreg. Pioneer Assn.* (1928): 57-64.

Dewolf, D., *Illinois State Historical Society* (1925): 183-222.
Dougherty, L. B., *Mo. Hist. Rev.* 24 (1930): 359-78, 550-67; 25 (1931): 102-51, 306-201, 474-89.
Findley, J. L., *Trans. Oreg. Pioneer Assn.* (1926): 23-25.
Gilliam, W. S., *Trans. Oreg. Pioneer Assn.* (1905): 411-23.
Helmick, S., *Oreg. Hist. Quart.* 26 (1925): 444-47.
Kelly, C., *Trans. Oreg. Pioneer Assn.* (1887): 52-63.
Lovejoy, A. L., *Oreg. Hist. Quart.* 31 (1930): 237-60.
Munger, A., *Oreg. Hist. Quart.* 8 (1907): 387-415.
Packwood, W., *Oreg. Hist. Quart.* 16 (1915): 33-54.
Parker, I. E. A., *Trans. Oreg. Pioneer Assn.* (1928): 17-35.
Parrish, E. E., *Trans. Oreg. Pioneer Assn.* (1888): 82-121.
Spencer, L., *Trans. Oreg. Pioneer Assn.* (1887): 74-78.
Tuller, M. A., *Trans. Oreg. Pioneer Assn.* (1895): 87-90.
Welch, N. D., *Trans. Oreg. Pioneer Assn.* (1897): 97-103.
Whitman, M., *Oreg. Hist. Quart.* 28 (1927): 239-57.

INDEX

Accidents, 90

Ague. See Malaria

Amputating instruments, 49

Artists, 19–20

Ashley, General William Henry, 23

Applegate, Jesse, expedition of 1843, 13; description of life on the trail, 53

Barlow, Samuel K., trail to Oregon City, 32

Bartleson, John, captain of Oregon expedition in 1841, 11, 15

Bartleson-Bidwell expedition, 11

Bathing and Baths, problems on trail, 62–63

Bennett-Arcane party, 96

Bidwell, John, 11

Bierstadt, Albert, artist, *Nooning on the Platte*, 54

Blackhills. See Laramie Mountains

Blisters, 71

Bodmer, K., 19

Bonneville, Captain Benjamin, 23

Bridger, James, exploits of, 14–15

Bruff, J. Goldsborough, artist, *The Rabbit Hole Springs*, 88

Bullboat, description of construction by John Ball, 60

Buffalo, as food·source, 67

Burials, 79–80

Burnett, Peter H., letter, advice on wagons, 36

California Trail. See Overland Trail

Carson River, 32

Catlin, George, 19

Chiles, Joseph B., 11

Chimney Rock, 20

Chloroform, discovery of, 46

Cholera, deaths on the trail, 77; epidemics of in the United States, 75; symptoms, 75; treatments, 77–79

Colorado tick fever. See Mountain Fever

Conestoga Wagon. See Wagons, covered

Cooking, how done on the trail, 66

Coughs and Colds, treatment of, 83–84

Court House Rock, 20

Davy, Sir Humphrey, 46

Death-rate, in the United States in 1840s, 44

DeSmet, Father Pierre-Jean, in the Bartleson-Bidwell group, 11

Diets, deficiencies in, 67

Digger Indians, 98

Diseases, kinds of reported in 1830s, 47

Doctors, as emigrants in 1840s, 18; training of in 1840s, 44–45

Donner Party, 94–95

Drake, Daniel, classification of fevers, 47